MY PRIVATE LENNON

21ST CENTURY ESSAYS

David Lazar and Patrick Madden, Series Editors

My Private Lennon

EXPLORATIONS FROM A
FAN WHO NEVER SCREAMED

SIBBIE O'SULLIVAN

MAD CREEK BOOKS, AN IMPRINT OF
THE OHIO STATE UNIVERSITY PRESS
COLUMBUS

Mad Creek Books, an imprint of The Ohio State University Press.

Library of Congress Cataloging-in-Publication Data.
Names: O'Sullivan, Sibbie, author.
Title: My private Lennon : explorations from a fan who never screamed / Sibbie O'Sullivan.
Other titles: 21st century essays.
Description: Columbus : Mad Creek Books, an imprint of The Ohio State University Press [2020] | Series: 21st century essays | Includes bibliographical references. | Summary: "Autobiographical essays that explore how John Lennon and The Beatles influenced the intellectual and artistic development of the author. Explores the musical, cultural, and personal aspects of intense music fandom"—Provided by publisher.
Identifiers: LCCN 2019034760 | ISBN 9780814255667 (paperback) | ISBN 0814255663 (paperback) | ISBN 9780814277584 (ebook) | ISBN 0814277586 (ebook)
Subjects: LCSH: O'Sullivan, Sibbie. | Lennon, John, 1940–1980—Influence. | Beatles—Influence.
Classification: LCC PS3565.S898 Z46 2020 | DDC 818/.603 [B]—dc23
LC record available at https://lccn.loc.gov/2019034760

Cover design by Angela Moody
Text design by Juliet Williams
Type set in Adobe Sabon

♾ The paper used in this publication meets the minimum requirements of the American National Standard for Information Sciences—Permanence of Paper for Printed Library Materials. ANSI Z39.48-1992.

This book is dedicated to the ladies
Verlyn Flieger
Fiona J. Mackintosh
Cynthia Matsakis
Sarah Pleydell
Linden von Eichel

CONTENTS

JOHN LENNON RETURNS HOME FROM HAMBURG TO AUNT MIMI'S IN LIVERPOOL, DECEMBER 8, 1960

There are no photographs but someone must have seen you, a column
of hunched anger carrying all that was dear, your amp and guitar, the few
biscuits Astrid tucked inside your leather coat. From one sea to another,
fear and hunger fear and hunger like the silence on the foreign trains,
the English tram, you too tired for anything except the narrow bed you'd
fall into.

She wouldn't let you in; she makes you wait, pebble after pebble
on the window pane. So you waited in the garden, for there was no place
else to go. She takes her time, knowing nothing of the calluses
your fingers bear, the amp, the honey-horned guitar you carried
like a shield but now lay down upon the gravel.

There's a lesson she wants you to learn that explains the sudden light,
an opening just enough for you to see her face, a face that would
outlive your own. "I told you so," it says, and the doorway widens.
Gathering the ragged amp, your bruised guitar, you step into the future
where a girl and her listening heart wait for you.

ASK ME WHY

The man who fixed my washing machine was writing out the bill when he saw the postcard photograph of John and Yoko on my bookshelf. The usual Beatles conversation ensued and then, because I couldn't help it, I blurted, "I was there."

"You were there?" By the incredulous tone of his "there" I'm pretty sure he thought I'd been at the photo shoot. Oh, what an experience that would have been, and questions like his can make liars of us all. But I'm a bad liar, so I told him the truth.

"I was there in the audience for their third Ed Sullivan show, August 1965, I saw them live."

"Wow, you did?" his eyes widening. Leaning toward me he asked more questions: No, I didn't scream; yes, Paul debuted "Yesterday." I also told him how I kept the ticket stub for decades before selling it to a connoisseur of Beatles memorabilia. But the photo of John that I took with my you-can-hold-it-in-one-hand Instamatic camera is forever tucked away in a safe place. For my eyes only.

There's something luxurious about remembering. It's such a private activity. It's often willed, and that sets it apart from dreaming, which is even more private. To remember is to know you have *been*. My small photograph of John on Ed Sullivan's stage doesn't give me the visual oomph that watching the full concert on YouTube does, but it is proof that I was there. Lately, I've been doing a lot of remembering. And dreaming.

My first indelible Beatles moment occurred when I was fifteen. That Anglophile T. S. Eliot pretty well sums it up: "Everyone, I believe, who is at all sensible to the seduction of poetry, can remember some moment in youth when he or she was completely carried away by the work of one poet. What happens is a kind of . . . invasion." Substitute poetry and poet with the Beatles and you have me on a cold, rainy December night in 1963 hearing John Lennon's voice for the first time. It was an invasion, I was captured, but instead of being held prisoner, I was set free. I felt my life beginning.

Monday, December 8, 1980, is also indelible, as is the phone call from an ex-lover telling me John had been killed. On Tuesday, still stunned by his murder, I didn't attend my weekly group therapy session because I wanted to watch the news stories about his death. At the next session, the therapist criticized my absence, telling the group that she and her children had lit candles in John's memory and then got on with it. Candles! That was the last group therapy meeting for me. No New Age ritual could smooth over his death. I needed to be alone in front of the TV, watching clips of John and the Beatles. His body and voice had ceased to be, and I wanted to hold on to whatever I could of him.

Often people ask, what was it about the Beatles that made me love them? There's no single answer, but here are a few reasons that help explain their impact on me: Their songs punctured my loneliness; their voices stirred me; their faces delighted my eyes. These are typical reasons to love the group. But I also had a bone-deep conviction—the kind only an adolescent ignorant of the past but ultra-sure of the future could have—that the Beatles represented huge, important changes of sweeping dimensions, in a word, *history*, some-thing I hadn't given much thought to, not even when JFK was killed, nor when, two days later, Lee Harvey Oswald's live-on-TV murder interrupted the morning show I was watching.

The Beatles gave me a reason to enter the historical world, and when I did, I cultivated a privacy of mind in which to think about and listen to them, but also to contemplate Life. Because of the Beatles, I learned to reason and to create, to imagine the lives and histories of others, and, most impor-tant, I began imagining myself in new ways, all of which is qualitatively different from simply appreciating the good looks of four English lads. Over the decades my love of them distilled into something basic, as most important things in life tend to do after you've reached a certain age. Quite sim-ply, the Beatles make me happy. Notice the present tense; that's no mistake.

When I began writing about the Beatles, I quickly real-ized that I was writing a love story. All kinds of love, all with different stories—love of music, love of my family and my daughter, love of the English language, love of teachers and friends, love of men, and love of myself as an American girl and woman. At the center of these loves are the Beatles, and at the center of the love I feel for them is my love of John Lennon. This love, and the indelible moments it's inspired, has shaped my life, and continues to do so.

However, even before Lennon's death, the Beatles had begun to recede into the background. Life happens; you can't stay a teenager forever, and by 1970, when they broke up, my life had radically changed. But their importance never com-pletely disappeared, nor did their music. They're the reason I visited England in 1986 to soak up the English experience and its varying accents, yet when I reached Liverpool, the only Beatles-related moment I had was a drive-by of the Cav-ern Club seen from the window of a cab. Seeing the house where John grew up seemed so cliché, and any official tour of the sites would disrupt the privacy in which I held him. Thinking about it now, I must have been paralyzed by self-consciousness, though it's also possible I put myself above those fans who unembarrassedly sought out the holy Beatles' locations. I stayed only one night in Liverpool, as I was travel weary and lonely. Now, of course, I could kick myself for leaving the city so soon.

What brought me back to John and the others? This return, which occurred gradually, interests me as much as my original feelings for them. As a girl, my daughter Kim began giving me Beatles gifts—photographs, T-shirts, books. She seemed to know something I didn't, because with each gift, not only was I touched but I became curious. Who was I when I first saw that photograph? Where was I? These questions merged with other, more present concerns: Would people think I was like a Trekkie if I went to work wearing the Imagine T-shirt Kim gave me, or should I just wear it around the house? Should a teacher in a university even wear a rock star T-shirt on campus? I was overthinking a piece of clothing, not sure of how its symbolism would look on me, but I knew absolutely the importance of the symbol.

In the late 1980s, I began to meet men who loved the Beatles as much as I did, along with one who didn't. Kevin, the man I sold my ticket stub to, was a record collector and involved in Beatles memorabilia. I showed him my photo of John, and he told me I could sell that too, if the time ever came. Hasn't come yet. Though my photograph of John is gray and small, I knew I had something others might want, a specific moment in history, but it was also a moment in my history. Knowing this has kept me close to John, even though I've tucked him away in a small drawer I seldom open.

Then there were the books. No overthinking there, as I'd been collecting books about music since high school. Kim gave me Philip Norman's *John Lennon: The Life* and later Mark Lewisohn's *The Complete Beatles Chronicles*. In 2013, after my first knee surgery, Lewisohn's *Tune In: The Beatles:*

All These Years took away the pain of recovery. Since 1968, I've owned Hunter Davies's official biography of the Beatles, but it can't compete with the newer ones. Once I began writing about the Beatles, I read many more books about them and rock music in general. Dylan's *Chronicles,* the assorted rock criticism I had by Lester Bangs, Dave Marsh, and Robert Christgau; Patti Smith's resonant *Just Kids*; the radical pronouncements of Greil Marcus; and Geoffrey O'Brien's stately essays were all pulled from my bookshelves with regularity, read and re-read, as were John's interviews with *Rolling Stone* and *Playboy.*

Ellen Willis's essays reminded me of how few women write about music, let alone the Beatles, and I thought that maybe I could help rectify that. Devin McKinney's *Magic Circles: The Beatles in Dream and History* convinced me there was an audience for subjective, even obtuse books about the Beatles, and that being subjective is fine, being obtuse not so much. Robert Christgau's recent memoir *Going into the City* is a mix of autobiography, criticism, and chest thumping. If he can write about the operation he had on his testicle, then, by golly, I could write about men's bodies, too. I could write a linear history, or a loopy one. I could write in different styles, get off my subject or get lost in it, even forget how important Beatles history is to me. I could use poems and photographs. Regardless of how or where I sliced this history, John Lennon was at the quick of it, and if I wanted to reach *my* John Lennon, I would have to reach deep into myself.

In *Retromania: Pop Culture's Addiction to Its Own Past,* Simon Reynolds analyzes the "re" phenomenon: the "*reviv*als, *re*issues, *re*makes, [and] *re*enactments" evident in popular culture, especially in pop music. Reynolds sees our world "obsessed with the cultural artifacts of *its own immediate past,*" and he's right: we are retro. We want to go back, to re-experience, and to do so consciously. Advances in technology allow this to happen. On YouTube I can *relive* my Ed Sullivan experience, letting, in Reynolds's words, "the moment become a monument." In writing these essays, I've indulged in what Reynolds terms "reflective nostalgia," an emotion-driven "bittersweet" reverie about a past that's "irrecoverable." That's me, ready for my close-up. But this kind of reliving only goes so far.

The fact that the Beatles as a group are irrecoverable takes nothing away from the thrill of listening, again and again, to their music. Though I originally played their albums on a small, portable mono phonograph, I don't long for its return, or regret that it's been replaced by better, more advanced technology. I love the remastered CDs of the Beatles' albums. Inheriting a Sony amp, a CD player, and two 901 Bose speakers has also facilitated my reverie. After reading Ian MacDonald's *Revolution in the Head,* a sublime analysis of every song the Beatles recorded, I became a fanatical listener. When I have my Walkman on, I can feel John's voice *inside* my head, something I couldn't experience as a teenager, and the precision and musical intricacy of their songs are now clearer and more evident. The Beatles are present on the CDs through their voices, just as they were on the earlier albums, which is how the majority of their fans initially experienced them. What can't be relived or reconstituted are the multitudinous experiences that created the *in situ* context in which we first heard those voices. Best to let the past be the past and resist retromania through private listening. But this might be easier said than done.

Recently, when the Fab Faux, bassist Will Lee's band that meticulously reproduces the Beatles repertoire, appeared in Washington, DC, I went and saw them. The night I went, the band played songs written or sung by John Lennon; the following night they played Paul's. It was a great show, the musicianship top-notch, and the audience seemed mesmerized with happiness. By the end I was almost in tears, but not for the past, not even for the original Beatles, who wouldn't have sounded nearly as good as Lee's band did, but for the absence of John Lennon's voice. For as good as the singing was, no one in the band could duplicate John's voice. How could they? And to their credit, they didn't try. A perfectly sung note, a note-perfect guitar lick played on what looked like the same make of guitars John, Paul, and George played, but no "If I Fell" or "I'll Be Back," two of John's most individualistic songs. Since December 8, 1980, the only way to hear John's voice is through a recording, a technology that keeps alive one part of him but not the whole. And that part, however grateful we are for having it, can't help but remind us of his absence. I was happy to hear the Fab Faux play John's songs live, but without John's voice, these songs also reminded me of his death.

To be captured by a voice is to be captured by time. Today, the Beatles are more present in my life than they were when I first heard them precisely because I am remembering them. Listening to them with adult ears, both feet on the ground and no teenage trembling, has made me *re*consider what it means when I say "I was there," and in the process I've learned that I can be "there" in multiple ways, that "there" can be many places at once, both past and present. So, let's go there.

BOYS

In her 1925 essay "How One Should Read a Book," Virginia Woolf takes on teachers and critics of literature by calling them "the gowned and furred authorities," which they were back then, wafting along the sidewalks of Cambridge and Oxford in their billowing academic robes and masses of facial hair. Woolf then urges readers to discount authority by respecting the "demon in us who whispers, 'I hate, I love,' whenever we read . . . because 'I hate, I love'" is "so intimate . . . we find the presence of another person intolerable." This is good advice.

When I was in graduate school getting my PhD, my professors were neither "gowned" nor "furred," and none would have sanctioned a dissertation based on such subjective protocol as "I hate, I love." But a hunch is not necessarily subjective, especially if it's well-researched and comes with footnotes. The hunch I had about Ernest Hemingway turned out to be right, and despite the dismissals I received from male readers, beginning with my dissertation director forbidding me to acknowledge him if my work got published, my ideas became part of the new wave of Hemingway criticism focusing on masculinity and gender. I had taken on the big boys and survived.

In academia, the markers of success are tenure and publication, and I've had none of the first and some of the second, which can result in deep self-doubt when certain tenured colleagues suggest in various weaselly ways I've no business teaching literature in a university. Whenever this happened, and, sadly, it did, I'd take solace in the fact that John Lennon was plagued by self-doubt all his life. I especially like to brood upon his 1964 experience when Foyles bookstore honored him at its annual Literary Luncheon for his book *In His Own Write*. Foyles expected John to give a speech, but he didn't know this. According to Cynthia Lennon's memoir *John,* he was "ashen and totally unprepared . . . [and] the weight of expectations was enormous." Terrified, all John managed to say was, "Thank you very much, it's been a pleasure," which was met with "stunned silence." He made up for it, though, by signing autographs. One woman was overheard saying how she "never thought [she'd] stoop to asking for such an autograph." John retorted, "And I never thought I would be forced to sign my name for someone like you," a comeback full of Liverpudlian sass and class leveling, something that would never occur in an American university without deep repercussions. When my dissertation director warned me not to use his name, I could not have replied, *Why do you think I ever would, you tosser?*

But it's John's speechlessness I most identify with. Silence haunted me in graduate school, not in my classes, but in the expected networking and give-and-take between professors and students. I was terribly worried that I'd mispronounce a term or someone's name, or make an unrecoverable mistake. Literary conferences were excruciating for me. I felt like an alien who had left all her protective gizmos back on the spaceship, and if I just clung to the corners or sat in the same chair all afternoon maybe no one would notice how out of it I was. I've experienced this sinking feeling from time to time throughout my life, so no harm in admitting it. I haven't permanently sunk, I haven't drowned; I'm not a loser, there are just certain things I'm not very good at.

The Beatles' sass was just a small part of the larger social changes occurring in the '60s. Though early rock and roll and postwar teen culture had upset the status quo, the Beatles phenomenon established a new one. The band's impact helped create a cultural mashup, a masscult leveling of surprising power and reach. At first, like millions of other teenagers, I experienced this mashup without being fully conscious of it. But by the end of 1964, I understood the larger cultural power that the Beatles exerted. By 1966, I realized that this mashup included some "gowned and furred authorities" of its own, the established classical music critics and composers who championed the Beatles. In 1963, William Mann of the London *Times* had declared his admiration for the band in a review containing his infamous statement about Aeolian cadences. With the release of *Sgt. Pepper's Lonely Hearts Club Band* in 1967, critics lauded the Beatles as capital "A" Artists, a promotion the band neither sought nor needed. In a 1968 essay for *The New York Review of Books*, composer Ned Rorem claims to have been "torn from a long antiseptic nap by the energy of rock," then goes on to compare Beatles music to such longhair composers as Monteverdi, Schumann, and Poulenc. Even as a teenager, I knew how irrelevant Rorem's argument was because John and Paul didn't know these composers. Obviously, Rorem needed to lash the Beatles' songs to the mast of classical precedents, a yoking young Beatles fans would have thought superfluous.

I knew of Leonard Bernstein, as many did. He conducted the New York Philharmonic, wrote the music for *West Side Story*, lectured about music on TV, had killer hair and a suave way with cigarettes. My father once chatted with him about Mahler, and that story lit up our household for a few days. I believe Bernstein admired the Beatles, but I have a hunch his admiration was also self-serving. He wasn't so much "gowned and furred" as intellectually cool in his cashmere turtleneck. When he proclaimed the Beatles' music "more adventurous than anything else written in serious music today," what was he really saying? In this context, "serious music" means contemporary classical, so to fully appreciate the absurdity of Bernstein's statement, it helps to remember that Aaron Copland was still writing in the 1960s, as were Samuel Barber, Duke Ellington, Luciano Beiro, Pierre Boulez, and Frank Zappa. What does Bernstein mean by "written," because the Beatles could neither read nor write music. Though they had George Martin's help with arrangements, they chose their own melodies and instrumentation in relatively primitive ways: by whistling, banging chords on pianos, test-driving harmonies and guitar riffs in the studio, and, on one occasion, asking Martin to create "orange sounds." These are not the methods of classical composers, and Bernstein knew it. His false equivalencies *elevate* the Beatles' musicianship closer to Bernstein's own. Though I've always been suspicious of older critics needing to qualify the Beatles, I understand it. Like millions of teenage girls, Bernstein and Rorem were making the Beatles their own.

For Bernstein, this elevation also worked in reverse: if the Beatles could be considered classical composers, why couldn't classical conductors gyrate like rock and rollers? With his own long hair (though not as long as the Beatles') and dramatic movements, Bernstein's conducting style had more in common with Pete Townshend's windmill guitar playing than with Toscanini's polite baton. Bernstein admired The Who and once secured a gig for them at Tanglewood. Nor is it outlandish to suggest that John and Yoko's 1969 bed-in for peace inspired the cocktail party Bernstein threw for the Black Panthers at his Park Avenue duplex the following year. Political swag was in style in the late '60s, but only Bernstein's event inspired a new phrase that encapsulated the cultural mashups yet to come: *radical chic.* Ironically, perhaps the most significant moment in this bidirectional cultural mashup wasn't middle-aged luminaries like Bernstein going gaga over *Sgt. Pepper* but the *negative* review of the album written by then-twenty-three-year-old Richard Goldstein for *the New York Times*. Rock criticism was a-birthin'. In 1966, one year before Goldstein's critique, *Crawdaddy* had hit the stands, soon to be followed by *CREEM* and later by *Rolling Stone*. The writers for these new publications didn't need classical precedents to validate their opinions. Rock and roll music now had its own niche and legitimacy, and critics and readers were free to love or hate whomever they chose, something that's continued to this day.

The big boys of Beatles criticism are a well-informed, lushly stylized, and sometimes combative group of men who know their stuff and stake out their territory regarding the music, politics, and personalities of the group. These critics advanced the cultural importance of the Fab Four and of pop music in general. The history of the Beatles is taught in universities and read by millions outside the classroom. Histories of the band are obviously important, and readers, including myself, await volume two of Mark Lewisohn's definitive research about the band. But historians and biographers are generally more neutral about their subjects than are rock critics who tend to write in pronounced styles, to which their readers respond in equally personal ways. No one disputes that Lester Bangs had a personality and that his prose style, the equivalent of a guitar power solo rumbling across the page, is the surest demonstration of it. But Bangs did not like the Beatles; he simply wrote them off: "The Beatles were four yobs, or rather three yobs and a librarian named Paul . . . The Beatles were nothing." Typical of most drug users, Bangs neglects the past because he's fixated on the future, his next pill or bottle of Romilar, so it's no surprise that he overlooked the delicious irony that were it not for those "nothing" Beatles rock criticism would never have happened, and Bangs, a pudgy kid from San Diego, would have probably remained just another syrup head dying from an overdose as everyone assumed he would and, finally, did. This may be harsh, but the word "yobs" really gets to me. Nevertheless, it's impossible to dismiss Bangs's contribution to rock criticism.

On the Internet, readers and fans don't hold back their opinions. Dave Marsh, an early writer for *CREEM* and now an established maven of rock history, is a "grumpy rock and roll journalist." Poor Dave. On Steve Hoffman's online Music Forum, there's a continuing debate over who's the best rock critic of all time. Some hate Bob Christgau but love Greil Marcus. Immodest Christgau drops names and political theories and likes to strut his street cred, while Berkeley-bred Marcus is the master of voodoo hermeneutics, wherein he fuses outlandish examples so expertly into his argument that the reader might take them on trust were they not so ridiculous. For example, is the opening of the Drifters' "*There Goes My Baby*" really comparable to "Lincoln [explaining] justice to a crowd . . . in 1832"? Like Bernstein and Rorem before them, Marcus and Christgau want to haul rock and roll up the cultural ladder, which is fine, but some of their arguments probably leave their lesser-schooled readers gasping for air on the lower rungs. Nevertheless, like Bangs, they are required reading. Others argue that my favorite, Ian MacDonald, is the best critic.

Sometimes a photograph is worth a thousand words, sometimes not. I'm fascinated by the only photo I found of MacDonald online. Posed with one hand on his hip, half his face in shadow, he exudes a Heathcliffian challenge, a photo of a man comfortable with his own contradictions. But who knows for sure? Everything I know about him I found on Wikipedia: born 1948 as Ian MacCormick in London, one year at Cambridge, wrote for *New Musical Express,* wrote a book on Shostakovich, was working on a book about nature symbolism when, at age 54, he committed suicide. Nothing I've read, even his obituaries, reveals how or why he killed himself, but his death is a great loss to music criticism. Mac-

Donald dedicates *Revolution in the Head* TO SHE WHO KNOWS, a shout-out with a particular Victorian valence. Who is this mystery woman? Why not name her? Did she spend time with his brain? Could I have spent time with his brain, or would he have waved me away with one flick of his beautifully posed left hand? Compared to MacDonald, American rock critic Bob Christgau doesn't challenge the camera and tends to dress casually, reflecting the anti-glamour of grunge, or the I-couldn't-care-less sartorial creed of old vinyl nerds. But I'd have to make a private tour of his closet to be sure.

Despite his casualness of dress, on the page Christgau can come across as pompous. The title of his memoir *Going into the City: Portrait of the Critic as a Young Man* broadcasts how seriously he wants his effort to be ranked with James Joyce's. As the self-proclaimed "dean of American rock critics," Christgau often writes assumptively about his experiences in the '60s and '70s, as though the entire country were involved in his counterculture ventures, and after a while his use of "we" becomes coercive. Compared to Christgau's, MacDonald's style is stately. His take on the '60s is more sociological, and certainly less mythic, but then '60s England was less mythic than '60s America. After reading both men, I have the impression that Christgau likes his brain a little too much, whereas MacDonald seems to struggle to keep his under control. Unlike some American critics (e.g., Bangs, Marcus) whose paragraphs tend to wander, however interestingly, MacDonald's are pinned to the page with the fastidiousness of a monastic scribe.

MacDonald, Marcus, and Christgau are the best critics in my opinion, though certain of their arguments can rile me. I'm not the only reader who wonders what MacDonald has against George Harrison. Criticism should never play to the common denominator, but it shouldn't be purposefully silly or esoteric either. Sometimes you just have to point out the idiocy in certain writers' work. Tim Riley has an aggravating tendency to psychoanalyze Beatles lyrics, especially John's. Depending on which song Riley is discussing, John can be inadequate, helpless, feeling profound fear, sounding drugged up, needing absolution, or "venting the hideously neurotic side of his sexual conditioning." I wonder how Riley would assess a Screamin' Jay Hawkins song? In all of this supposed angst, the true value of John's singing gets lost.

In his book *Magic Circles: The Beatles in Dream and History*, Devin McKinney relies on an updated version of the excremental vision to entice his readers, but many will just be disgusted. McKinney exclaims, "The toilet is the essence of rock . . . the sound of the toilet circles back again and again." Rock and roll is an "agglomeration of fluids . . . it slithers from juke joints on back roads . . . the natural product of tight, dim places . . . so many recoiled when the Great American Toilet yielded this funk." Though McKinney goes on to say many astute things in his book, compared to MacDonald's evenness or Christgau's cultural weavings, *Circles* makes one unnecessarily dizzy with too many ditzy statements.

Having said all this about the boys of rock criticism, who am I to talk, given the dearth of my own critical efforts? My first, and last, foray into music criticism was in high school: in Mr. Diggs's twelfth-grade semantics class, I gave a brief but pungent oral presentation on the poetry of the blues. Regardless of how seriously I researched, pouring over Paul Oliver's *Blues Fell This Morning* (later retitled *The Meaning of the Blues*) and other sources, my report ended up being a ribald litany of the sexual metaphors I could explain and share via my record collection. The class LOVED it. Until my friend Kevin gave me a copy of Greil Marcus's *Mystery Train: Images of America in Rock 'N' Roll Music* in the late 1980s, I'd done little serious reading about rock and roll, devoting myself instead to literary works. I hadn't yet formed a theory of what it meant to love the Beatles, nor did I discover a critical fulcrum from which to rebalance existing ideas about the band, as I later did with Hemingway. Listening to the Beatles and reading about them was enough. But because I was trained to examine works of art through frames other than the personal, the Beatles and their history began to slowly mesh with my own scholarly interests about masculinity, the body, and American culture. Consequently, I began reading the Beatles in critical ways. But after fifty years of Beatles criticism, is there anything left to say?

Even if I wanted to dismantle the grand narrative of the fifteen-year-old female Beatles fan, I couldn't do it. That thousands of hysterical girls screamed at the Beatles is a fact, and, like it or not, because I was a teenage female fan, I'm subsumed into this hysteria. *Did you scream?* is the first thing I'm asked when men learn I saw them live. No male Beatles fan or rock critic suffers this conundrum. The pitiful ratio of females to males who have written about the band does nothing to relieve this conundrum either. The late Ellen Willis, who wrote astutely about '60s music, admits she screamed during rock concerts, but only so she wouldn't be "conspicuous," which isn't much of an analysis of what the screaming might have meant.

I have no idea what this hysteria meant. Sure, it's collective behavior, and many see it as sexually driven, which, unfortunately, is the historically fraught explanation for *all* unconventional female behavior. But what's so sexual about blubbering and peeing your pants? Viewing young female sexuality this way is demeaning. As boys, as young teens, John and Paul participated in circle jerks with their male buddies. Circle jerks are collective, sexual, and involve a certain fluid, but you wouldn't want to have a circle jerk in Shea Stadium; it would give teenage boys a bad name. See where I'm going with this?

The image of the young hysterical Beatles fan has been essentialized, depersonalized, and inadequately explained. "The girls are subconsciously preparing for motherhood," we read in Philip Norman's *Shout! The Beatles in Their*

Generation. "Their frenzied screams are a rehearsal for that moment. Even the Jelly Babies (the candies favored by the early Beatles and hurled at them by fans) are symbolic." To steal a line from Greil Marcus, *What is this shit?* How can giving birth, a one-of-a-kind physical phenomenon, be rehearsed in advance? Only a man could suggest such a thing. The American version of Jelly Babies is jelly beans, and they aren't symbolic of children. To the Beatles, these candies were very material, and George Harrison is on record asking fans not to throw them because they hurt and stuck to the stage.

I find Barbara Ehrenreich's theory more palatable. For her, the screaming "was, in form if not in conscious intent, to protest the sexual repressiveness, the rigid double standard of female teen culture. It was the first and most dramatic uprising of women's sexual revolution." This argument at least gives the screaming girls agency, as their force was directed outward toward a specific other, unlike the circle jerk which, despite being communal, is ultimately self-referential. Consequently, when girls screamed for the Beatles, their social power needed to be contained, and it was, by barricades, policemen, and bouncers who patrolled the concert venues.

Another facet of Beatles criticism I can't fathom is the claim they were androgynous. Were they truly androgynous or were they simply impeccably tailored beautiful Englishmen? When you feminize the Beatles, you dilute the power of male beauty and limit what's acceptably masculine. I'm pretty sure that in 1964 few teenage girls knew what androgyny was—I certainly didn't. What the Beatles' hairstyle and dress did do was loosen and expand ways straight men could look. Long hair, stylish boots, jeans, flowing shirts, colors for god's sake, rapidly became de rigueur.

If teenage girls screamed when the Beatles shook their heads, they could have simply been responding to seeing hair actually move, given how flat-topped, greased up or encased in military-grade hairspray American hair had become by 1964. Imagine running your hands through a Beatle's hair, pulling it back off his forehead! There'd be a big payoff in that: their faces, and what fabulous faces they were—real, released from cosmetics, flawed. Consider the inside fold-out photo on the *Beatles for Sale* CD: their heads and brows covered by hair, their necks by coat collars, but the band's faces are a revelation. Intense and challenging, all unsmiling; no one would use the term "boy band" to describe these faces, as they clearly belong to men, their smoky, mysterious power capable of arresting the viewer.

The Beatles gave themselves over to the observer. One power a fifteen-year-old female fan had was the power to look, to stare, to *gaze,* to be transfixed by male beauty, something "good" girls only did in private. Only boys could openly assess girls, which accounted for why my best friend Betty and I had to develop our private code, the *bbbBB*s, in order to crotch watch. But Beatlemania permitted the power and utility of the female gaze to become hugely public. When female teenage Beatles fans asked one another who's your favorite Beatle, it was another version of one man asking another, *Are you a leg or a breast man?* But with one big difference. Teenage girls were invested in the *entire* Beatle body—face, teeth, hair, hands, voice, eyes, gesture, smile— before they extracted specific parts upon which to base their choice, though some probably made instinctive, unexamined choices as well. Either way, the fans' eyes led the way, and compared to homegrown teen idols who tended to look and sound alike, the Beatles gave the American girl lots to consider.

In a live format, the Beatles seemed comfortable with the female gaze. Bowing after every song seemed to condone it. Paul, especially, played to the screams in adolescent ways, batting his eyelashes, sending a smile to the balcony and handling his guitar more aggressively than either John or George, so maybe there is something to this androgyny after all; if so, it's specific to Paul. But live concerts are ephemeral. In the absence of YouTube or MTV, still photographs commanded the female gaze, allowing fans to create private fantasies that concerts couldn't, fantasies that could change over time, just as the Beatles themselves did. By collecting images of the Beatles, teenage girls were constructing a sense of self that accommodated their wishful narrative until the real world proved it false or irrelevant. What's important is the rupture, the giving up of fantasy, or transforming the youthful frenzy into something of greater meaning, and I don't mean getting married or having a child, though a woman's choice of a partner could very well be influenced by her teenage frenzy. The fantasies that do lasting damage are the kind that Mark David Chapman held on to.

So instead of asking a woman if she ever screamed for the Beatles, ask instead what she did with the love she had for them. Did it make her a specific kind of individual? If so, what kind? If all she says is *The Beatles made me happy when I was young,* that's sufficient. We need to hold on to all our happinesses regardless of when they happened or what caused them. We need to know what we love.

IN MY LIFE

John and the Beatles

My loyalty sometimes disgusts me. But that's how love works: lightning strikes, an arrow pierces the heart, the ground shakes and opens. Either way you're a goner, gone for good. I'm like one of those orphaned birds that imprints on a hang glider or a benevolent drone: *Take me with you. I'm yours for life.*

Falling in love with John Lennon was like that. Bereft in the usual teenage ways, teasing the shit out of my hair while inadvertently huffing Aqua Net in the hormonal bog of the girls' bathroom in my junior high, I would soon be captivated by something in the air that came and claimed me.

It was a cold, rainy evening in December 1963. Betty, Diane, and I walking close together listening to Betty's transistor radio. When the deejay announced that the new Beatles record was upcoming, we stopped and huddled closer. Then we heard "I Want to Hold Your Hand" and "I Saw Her Standing There."

I remember the scene only one way: *a widening overhead shot of three bodies forming a circle, shoulders drawn close, heads bent, someone holding up an umbrella. The suburban street, the houses, the air itself glistening with rain falling through the golden beam of the street light.*

Did I experience this magic moment as though I were directing it, making sure it would remain in my mind as a shot from a movie? If so, then this is the high-angle shot of me falling in love with a voice, a voice that would change my life.

I was certainly ready for a change. My hair couldn't take much more teasing, and I was fed up with the rinky-dink songs that dominated the airwaves. I was even getting tired of Dion, whom I liked. But it was the Four Seasons who really grated my sensibilities with all their falsetto exclamations. I once scorched a white cotton blouse with a cute sailor collar because, in rushing to turn off the radio, I forgot to lift the iron. *Sherrr-iii-eee* could kiss my ass, though I didn't quite think in those terms back then.

My style in men was changing, too. Let me repeat that: my style in men was changing, too, as though I actually knew something about men, or even teenage boys. For a while, I ogled the American tough, those junior-high-size Stanley Kowalskis of my youth who cuffed their cigarettes in the rolled-up sleeves of their white T-shirts. One in particular, a boy called Buzzy, was rumored to have sixteen-inch biceps. That sounds quaint today, what with eighth graders sending selfies and planning lipstick parties, but back in the early '60s, being a tough was better than being a dork, and muscles mattered, as they signaled protection and a readiness for violence. The tough girls knew this better than I ever would. When Gail, Buzzy's girlfriend, showed me the butcher knife she carried in her shoulder bag, I nearly fainted. If I became Buzzy's girl, would I also have to carry kitchen cutlery in my purse? Despite my trembling worries, I stuck with the toughs; I figured I might learn something useful for later on, after the trembling stopped.

At teen club, everybody danced to the same records: "I Can't Stop Loving You," "Sheila," the Isley Brothers' "Twist and Shout," "Stranger on the Shore," and the Cookies'

"Don't Say Nothing Bad About My Baby." But I hankered for a change, musically and otherwise. I'd be in high school soon. The toughs would drop out when they turned sixteen or else descend into the basement curriculum of automotive mechanics, never to be seen again. And I wasn't keen on the surfer look—too blonde and madras-y and, musically, way too white. So, in 1963, I was primed for John Lennon to point his Liverpool-tough musical finger at me and say, *'Ello, luv, how 'bout it?* and off I went like an orphaned goose.

People no longer huddle over transistor radios or tape recorders; that thrill is gone. There's no need to transcribe radio interviews in order to give a voice a second life on paper. But when Carroll James, a deejay at WWDC, a local Washington, DC, AM station, landed an interview with the Beatles before their first live American concert at the Washington Coliseum on February 11, 1964, Betty and I taped it. Then we painstakingly transcribed it. One wrong turn of a knob or press of a wrong button on the tape recorder and John, Paul, George, and Ringo would disappear into audio oblivion. Thanks to the Internet, I have listened online to that Carroll James interview, and hearing it again is more than a memory, it's a resurrection.

I come from a musical family. My father was a professional jazz musician touring with big bands throughout the late 1920s until 1942, when he joined the US Army Band. My mother, like many women of her generation, could play classical piano fairly well. I grew up listening to Louis Armstrong and Charlie Parker, and I didn't think their music was much different from Little Richard's "Keep A-Knockin'," my first 45 record. To my eight-year-old ear, all three performers produced high-energy basement jive capable of escaping upstairs to where the decent folk live, and it made no difference to me if the screaming came from an instrument or from a human voice. But when my mother snapped off the radio in the middle of Elvis's "All Shook Up," I knew rock and roll was my music and not my parents'.

And so it began: Elvis, Jerry Lee Lewis, Chuck Berry, Hank Ballard, Buddy Holly, Brenda Lee, and when I wasn't dancing around the house, I'd moon over the teen anthems of Paul Anka, Little Anthony and the Imperials, the Teddy Bears, and the Fleetwoods. Little did I know then that an ocean away the Beatles were listening to the same records I loved.

Unlike today, in the late '50s and early '60s, one could actually have a childhood. Parents used to caution, *What's your hurry, enjoy it while you can.* However, in order to speed things along, I saved my nickels and bought my first lipstick, Coral Luster by Charles of the Ritz, the summer before seventh grade. I had trading cards and a Hula-Hoop. But the mystery of the adult world still seeped in. To my young ears, Elvis's "Heartbreak Hotel" careened between madness and collapse, exposing shadowy precincts of adult pain I knew nothing about. Yet, somehow, I did know that there was more emotional truth in a W. C. Handy blues than in Mark Dinning's 1960 death-soaked "Teen Angel." Anyone can get run over by an oncoming train, but to have someone come after you with a razor is something else altogether. I knew certain songs contained an education if you really listened to them. Once the Beatles arrived, I learned that this applied to singers as well.

The question has always been *Are you a Paul or a John girl?* Betty was nuts for Paul, especially his eyes and curving brows. I adored John. Neither pretty like Paul's, nor classically handsome like Cary Grant's, John's face was tougher and full of surprises. I loved his chiseled nose, his narrow lips. There was a purity in John I didn't see in Paul, especially when Paul tilted his head and batted his eyes at any camera pointed his way. Much has been written about John's wide-legged stance while singing, some even suggesting his posture is an enticement to oral sex—please please me and all that—but it could simply be that, as the rhythm guitarist, he had to be vigilant about the song's momentum, and the best way to do that was to keep both feet firmly on the ground. I now appreciate the sexual speculation as my visual investment in John's body has been constant throughout the years. At fifteen, I didn't know what my eyes were telling me, or that in future years my body would seek out in other men specific physical traits that John possessed, most notably beautiful hands and a distinctive voice.

Betty and I never screamed. We preferred to ooze. On her bedroom wall, she had the poster for their 1963 show at the London Palladium. Positioned in a brick doorway, wearing topcoats, and only their faces and hands visible, J, P, G & R exuded both menace and respectability. Such limited bits of flesh on which to build a fantasy, but enough. Like Miranda in *The Tempest*, Betty and I gazed in wonder. And then we'd spend the day discussing J, P, G & R at length.

Any image that transfixes has power, even if those who are transfixed are fifteen-year-olds. That the Beatles were a musical quartet instead of athletes or politicians, men society expected to exude power and allure, added to their appeal and forcefulness. All *they* had to do to make the status quo shake and shimmy was open their mouths and move their fingers. From here on out, cultural power would belong to the young, the untrained, the shaggy-haired dreamers of postwar England and post-JFK America. But Betty and I weren't interested in contemporary cultural shifts. We were discovering how we loved and why. We were engaged in that ancient debate: Truth or beauty? John or Paul?

Though I loved songs by black male singers, I never hung a photograph of Smokey Robinson above my bed. Not because I knew my mother would have a fit, but because it never occurred to me to do so. Black male singers simply did not register on my gaze-o-tron. Instead, I *saw* them with my ears, evaluating them solely on their singing. No black singer seemed sexual to me. But, then, neither had Elvis, not even when he wore tight white swim trunks in *Blue Hawaii*.

It could have been the hairstyles, the conking and elaborate pompadours black singers had; they looked alien, futuristic. But so did Conway Twitty with his mile-high pompadour. What early stirrings I did have for males were sudden and unpredictable. Watching Marlon Brando in his undershirt in *A Streetcar Named Desire* created a certain tingle in as-yet-undiscovered places. And Kooky, the valet in *77 Sunset Strip*, got to me every time he took out his comb.

What did make me feel sexy was watching sexy women, especially those with big breasts: Marilyn, Jane, Diana Dors, Edie Adams selling White Owl cigars, Julie London emerging from the off-stage fog to sing "Cry Me a River" on a TV variety show. Pulp goddesses, the standard male version of female desirability, and I wanted to be desired, not to kiss so much as to be kissed.

It was different with the Beatles. By 1964, when they conquered America, my mind, like my bust, had expanded. I realize now that it had helped that John and I shared the same bloodline, Anglo-Irish. That genetic fact seemed to cancel any attraction I might have had to Otherness, whether Smokey Robinson's or Fabian's. John pushed an atavistic button in me, and I felt a recondite tribal pull. His face hypnotized me, and his voice, with its velvety nap, warm and tender on one side and rougher on the other, kept me in suspense. He was singing directly to me, and I believed every word regardless of whether they were venal, *give me money,* or deadly serious, as in *I nearly died,* the anguished *cri de coeur* of "No Reply."

Lennon's beauty converted me to new categories of masculine appeal. Now a long scarf, a booted foot, or a little cap caught my eye. Intelligence became sexy and redirected my teenage crushes toward a new class of boys: shy, awkward artist types; clever ones; savants who let their shirttails hang out. From this nexus I built my prototype: masculine but not muscled; musical, if possible; verbally astute; intelligent yet capable of landing a punch on a pesky adversary, if necessary.

But I was also dreaming of good hair, a good mouth, and what I'd now call a phallic presence, though I had had zip experience with anything phallic. Did I kiss my pillow and murmur *John* . . . or Robert or Dave? Probably. Did I practice kissing on my upper arm? All the time. Did I faint or scream when I saw the Beatles live in the Ed Sullivan studio on August 14, 1965? Definitely not. I hated the screamers. By then, the Beatles had produced a cascading effect on me, one that superseded sex. Hard to believe, I know, but art will do that to you.

The effect they had on me felt like an unexpected acceleration into the future. I suddenly knew what I wanted to be, to do, and what would give my life meaning. All of this newness made me think of an old Elvis song whose three ascending distinctions now made sense to me: *I want you, I need you, I love you.* I began to ask myself, what did *I* need? What did *I* love? These became my primary questions, and a good example of how language shapes human motive and behavior. From within my teenage frenzy, adult judgments, career decisions, and aesthetic endeavors began to form. Like John Lennon, I had fallen in love with words. Like John Lennon, I wanted to make something with them.

Transcribing the WWDC interview was the beginning. Betty and I were diligent scribes, carefully minding the tape recorder's capstan and the counter that indicated our stops and starts. Sometimes it was difficult to know which Beatle was speaking, especially when they commented among themselves. But accuracy might not have been our prime focus. Just hearing their voices was enough, four Englishmen speaking English.

How many times had I watched *Rebecca* on TV or seen movies where the butlers talked without moving their faces? Too many to remember. Betty and I used to parody their kind of British accent, our chins out, noses up, prancing around proclaiming *I say, old boy* or *Oh, but it's ghastly, simply ghastly.* But Betty and I had never heard anyone sound like George Harrison when, at the end of the interview, he said, *"I want to be a baggy swigger."*

Baggy swigger!? We knew it had to be something dirty because the others had laughed. So off I trotted to my local library to consult the biggest dictionary they had, the one on the wooden pedestal. Was that the day I decided to study literature and learned to enjoy the intricacies of scholarship? It seems trivial to say so. After all, we had a big dictionary at home, and I had already familiarized myself with my father's books. But researching the Beatles was fundamentally different; it felt necessary and often secretive. And though I figured millions of other teenage girls were researching as well, my endeavors felt intensely private. *Necessary, secret, private*—sounds like puberty, and in some ways I expect it was, my intellectual puberty.

Tracking down the meaning of George's comment lit a flame in me. I *had* to know. And the joy of discovering that filthy information could be found in my hometown library, that local tomb where silent, eagle-eyed women policed the stacks, was gleefully subversive. Once more I began to ooze, but this time it was over knowledge.

I discovered "baggage" is an old word for "prostitute." "Swigger" didn't produce any alternate definition, but after much giggling and hopping about, Betty and I reached our own conclusions: George wants to swig whores, slurp them, turn them upside down like a jug of whiskey! And he'd said so on the radio! We were in heaven. Elvis wouldn't have dared say anything like that.

Next, I read in some magazine that people compared John's prose to James Joyce's *Ulysses* and that Paul had read *The Miller's Tale* in high school. I think there was a reference to *Lady Chatterley's Lover,* too. It took some digging to learn that *The Miller's Tale* was not a novel but Chaucer's most infamous *Tale.* When I asked at the checkout desk for a copy of *Lady Chatterley's Lover,* a column of tweed rose up and coolly responded, *Young lady, that book is a restricted item.* OK, I thought, if I can't get the book, I can at least learn about the author, which began my D. H. Lawrence phase.

To get a running start on English history, I attacked the encyclopedias in the reference room, but there was so much information I did little except flip the pages and read the captions. In the stacks, I'd be sitting on the floor surrounded by books when a pair of shoes would suddenly appear beside me. The tomb police. *Find what you need?* she asked, then reminded me to put the book back on the cart and not the shelf when I was finished with it. A few times I "put the book back" inside my purse.

From the 770 shelf, photography, I found images of Liverpool, mostly of shipyards and blocks of wet brick houses. Enthralled, I imagined myself in that gray moist world, my collar turned up, leaning against a bombed-out wall practicing my French inhale. One day, I razored out a photograph of a handsome man in a pub sitting in a corner booth. I liked his face, so I took it home with me.

But despite my commitment to the Beatles, by the fall of 1964, I'd become a promiscuous listener of other bands and singers. I loved the British Invasion bands and bought many of their records, moving through the alphabet from the Animals to the Zombies. I especially loved the British blues bands and how incredibly cool it was that white boys were playing black American songs. At that time, I didn't realize that this transatlantic excavation of older black players and their songs was a watershed moment in modern material culture; I was just excited to discover new singers and songs whose lyrics overflowed with a poetic slang that made George Harrison's "baggy swigger" quaint in comparison.

Of course there was Dylan, exciting in both voice and face, but not in the complete way Lennon was. I loved Cream, once played their "Sunshine of Your Love" so loud the neighbors called the cops. If I loved the face of an unknown singer, I bought his album. That's how I acquired a life-long interest in Tom Rush, Tim Buckley, Bert Jansch, Dave Ray, and John Hammond Jr., the last posed like a schoolyard tough in a leather jacket sitting on a red Honda Superhawk. From high school I knew a ragtag group of budding blues guitarists, and they'd invite me to their jams and, *Oh, by the way, can you bring your albums?* So, yeah, I was a groupie, laden with LPs. I didn't mind; it gave me a credibility I enjoyed.

Some time in 1965, I began to throw out or give away my many Beatles magazines, with one exception, which I still have: a glossy package, *The Beatles*, photos by Norman Parkinson, with Words by Maureen Cleave, published by Hutchinson of London, 1964. It cost me 50 cents. Today on eBay it goes for about $20. I made room in my record cabinet for albums by different musicians, just as I had pushed aside my D. H. Lawrence books to make room for other authors. Soon I had hundreds of each. My post-high school world awaited me: crappy jobs, college, writing poetry, and, finally, though not too successfully, having sex.

And then, just like the Beatles, it all fell apart.

The story of the Beatles' demise is riveting, whereas my marrying the wrong man is not. Knowing nothing about men except that I wanted one, in 1970 I entered marriage naïve and pregnant. I was twenty-one. I knew immediately I'd made a grave mistake. Not a bad man by anyone's standards, but like Pete Best with the Beatles, my husband and I were a poor fit. We had books, and I'm pretty sure we had an old stereo, but I have no memory of playing my LPs while married. My husband's sole response to *Abbey Road* was to commend the lyrics to "She Came in Through the Bathroom Window" for being legally correct with regard to the criminal difference between rob versus steal.

After my divorce, my musical tastes often shifted according to whatever man I was with. One, a bully who enjoyed dragging me by the hair across his living room rug, loved Steely Dan. He used to stand on the coffee table and sing "Rikki Don't Lose That Number" while I sat nude on the couch. It was a kind of fun, I suppose, but one with a high cost.

Later, with another, it was all funk and R & B. Dancing till dawn in a black club quickly revealed my insufficiencies. Later, I had a jazz phase, still later a New Wave and early punk phase. But by then I was too old to pretend I liked what I was hearing. I moved on, leaving the black eyeliner to the boys with the spiked hair and steel-toed boots.

I don't know when I came back to the Beatles, but December 8, 1980, is as good a date as any. I was in bed when the phone rang. It was the hair dragger who almost ruined my life calling to tell me that John Lennon had been shot. It was the nicest thing he'd ever done.

Nostalgia says, *Things don't have to change.* Time says, *Oh, yes they do.* If I'm nostalgic for the Beatles, I'm also nostalgic for that girl who fell in love with them that rainy night in 1963. What good is memory if it can't convince us that the things we used to hold sacred or the people we used to be still matter? Can nostalgia also obstruct the truth of who the people we love really are?

Being a fan is like floating down a long river: some banks have lush vegetation, some are strewn with beer bottles, some are for sunbathing, around the next one there's a lovely sunset. The point is to *know* the river, to dip your foot in it as many times it takes to feel it as it moves along, which it will do with or without you. I've made a bargain with myself, granted, not too hard a one: in order to keep John's voice, I had to keep the man, all in all.

After reading Cynthia Lennon's second memoir, *John,* I was in a kind of stupor. I'd already heard about some of John's bad behavior, but I hadn't heard it from Cynthia. The wife: sweet, passive, protective, uncomplaining, holding the household together. Perhaps an angrier woman, or one whose writing talents were sharper, would have painted an even uglier portrait of a man loved by millions. Hers was enough for me. The book tested my loyalty in unexpected ways. If I disposed of John, threw him out of the pantheon, then I'd have to dispose of myself as well, or at least do some life-editing I wasn't prepared to do.

People do damage, geniuses probably more than the rest of us. Given John Lennon's history and early emotional scarring, it's surprising he didn't do more than he did. Instead, he made songs that have eased my own emotional debilities, and probably his, too.

Is there another art form that packs as much life force as does a good rock and roll record? In three minutes or less, you've got melody, rhythm, a human voice, and a story of love, death, desire, ecstasy, betrayal, money—all the plots of human experience—contained in a repeatable, cheap, transportable format, one that can sustain a person for a lifetime. To all this, John Lennon might laugh and say, *It's only rock 'n' roll, luv, you're makin' too big of it.* I'll never know for sure, but I think he'd agree with me.

MOTHER

Millions have seen the photograph: Julia Lennon in a print maternity dress holding her son John, one hand gripping his left biceps, the other dangling over his right shoulder, possibly tickling his armpit or upper chest (we don't speak of boys having breasts even if they do). This hand over John's shoulder is large, mannish, but the nails are brightly painted. She is claiming him, pulling him close. John is making one of his faces, squinching all his features in stark counterpoint to his mother's serene, full-faced offering. If we didn't know of John's penchant for making faces, we might read his distortions, along with his jabbing right hand, as resistance or annoyance at being captured by this woman who wears her wide-brimmed summer hat far back on her head cowboy style.

But we know he adores her, and she him, though they've lived apart for years.

He's almost nine, his body two angled arms and one sweet curve where the flesh of his exposed leg disappears up his summer shorts. His left shoulder rests below her right breast, which swells against her dress's second and third button. His left elbow presses into her thigh where it meets her lap. With shoulder and arm he's pressing against the secret place beneath his mother's cloak-like dress, the place of his long-ago beginning, origin of his first music, the sound of his mother's blood loving him.

This is the only photograph of John with his mother. It was taken in 1949 when John was eight. On July 15, 1958, she was killed by a drunk driver. John was seventeen.

We don't need Freud to tell us we're primed to feel lack; our bodies teach us this. The body of the mother, what my friend Sarah calls "the ground we come from," is our early bliss and our first wound. We learn that the breast is finite. To mature is to let go the dream of sucking on it. Breasts have a mystique. So why, after decades of looking at this photograph, have I never noticed Julia's breast pushing against her dress?

Looking at and writing about John gets me close to his body, but close to Julia's, too, as he might have seen and felt it, longed for it in various ways throughout his life. His mother's breasts, my mother's breasts, my own, right now pressing against my bent elbows as I type this sentence. Bliss and wound.

The mother's breast is so mysterious it's sometimes confined to silence, an excommunication from its natural state rendering it mute and invisible: Mary McCartney's breast, the one that killed her at age forty-seven, when her son Paul was fourteen. No one in that family mentioned the word: *cancer, cancer of the breast.* And Paul never asked. When told she had died, his response was, "What'll we do without her money?" They managed, father, younger brother, and Paul, a family now of men, a good family, but after Mary's death one without mystery, without breasts.

As I look through photographs of Liverpool, of the Beatles and their parents, their postwar world before electric guitars and new hairstyles changed everything, here's some of what I'm thinking about: differences in the amount of touching done in families; certain displays of affection within a family; who sat close together, who apart; hospital wards versus private rooms; backyard privies instead of indoor toilets; sweater girls; Jayne Mansfield in *The Girl Can't Help It* in 1957; Bridget Bardot; first base and finger pie; John's supposed loss of virginity at thirteen to an older woman; older women's breasts, the nursing mother, or the mother who would like to regain that lost paradise with her grown child.

Perhaps all this. Or perhaps something darker, manipulative and exploitive, something that didn't happen because John or Julia didn't let it. Two passive bodies with years between them, years of abandonment and yearning but also the commonality between parent and child. But then, over the years, the tensions of sex enter, tensions of bodily awareness, the son no longer a baby but a man, sexual, hungry in adult ways but waiting for a signal, a sure sign—*there!*, the three thoracic sympathetic nerves of the nipple—peaking his mother's sweater, poking up the cashmere—for it was cashmere, not a mohair sweater, as he first thought.

This memory is on a private audiotape John made in 1979. On it he confesses to desiring his mother but also to his confusion regarding that desire. It could happen to anyone, couldn't it; how easy it would be to reach across that small distance. *Son, forgive me for abandoning you,* and she places his hand where his baby mouth once was. *Mommy, I'm home, help me touch you without hurting us.* A mother places her son's hand on one of her breasts. Or he's placed his hand there, and she allows it. We can choose to see this as affection, factual bodily affection for the life-giving and life-long biological union between mother and child, or we can see it as something else.

The details he remembers are astonishing: the color of her sweater, the design in the skirt she's wearing. On the tape, John sounds drunk or perhaps on downers. We hear strange clicking noises, like he's eating a piece of hard candy. We don't know why he's making this tape, except that he was always making tapes of one sort or another. But this tape's subject is childhood sexual memories. Something has taken him back; or something that's never left him is beginning to itch again.

After his description of touching his mother's breast—he calls it her "tit," a syllable with bite—he describes another scene, one Freud called the primal scene, John's Wolf Man moment when he walks into the bedroom Julia shares with her common-law husband, Bobby Dykins, whom John referred to as Twitchy. Julia is beneath the sheets giving Twitchy head. John doesn't say if they saw him standing in the doorway, if Twitchy yelled "Get out!" or if his mother stayed hidden, her shoulders deflating beneath the sheet that hides her what— embarrassment, shame, aggravation? John sees, John knows, as he's been with girls for some time now. But he's bothered that his mum is doing *that* with Twitchy. We hear the disgust and heaviness in his adult voice, his original confusion pouring out as the memory drops farther back in his throat. Nothing, I'm sure, has prepared John for seeing his mother like this, but today, because of films and talk shows, this scene might warrant nothing more than an eye roll or a tossed off *whatever* before the door was shut again. For John, however, this scene needs to be memorialized, literally recorded, when he's thirty-nine years old.

Why shouldn't he remember this body in its cashmere sweater and colorful skirt? By all accounts Julia was beautiful; Paul described her as "a very beautiful lady, with long red hair," and comparing the photos of her to Mary McCartney we see that Paul was right. Julia was fun loving, musical, and witty—all the things John was. Like John, she had little use for convention. While still legally married to Alf Lennon, John's dad who had abandoned them, Julia publically "lived in sin" with Twitchy. She seemed not to care what others thought. Today we'd use other terms to describe her behavior: alcoholic, unfit mother, cougar. She clearly lived in the moment, and compared to her four sisters, all loving aunts to John, Julia was the black sheep of the Stanley clan. In interviews John states his admiration for these five strong women, the matriarchy he was raised in. Imagine all the female bodies that cuddled and kissed his, all the Yardley-scented bosoms he was smashed against. Bodily knowledge, not sexual, or at least not yet sexual, for as we grow up we conflate the two and learn that what we're feeling is often culturally taboo. On the same tape, John mentions reading about a man who's worried about having sexual fantasies in his 40s. John's worried, too, that the fantasies may never stop. They don't, not until we're dead.

When I was around twelve and not yet wearing a bra, I stood next to my father as he wrote music in one of the upstairs bedrooms. It was summer and I remember thinking how strange it was that my mother was in the hall vacuuming, as she seldom cleaned house. Daddy had his arm around my waist, explaining what he was doing on the score sheet spread out on the desk. Then he put his hand under my white blouse, quickly squeezed my right breast and said, "My girl is growing up." And that was that.

I don't know exactly what I felt, but certainly not revulsion. It didn't feel creepy, though I now know he shouldn't have done it. His squeeze was factual: I *was* developing, and he seemed pleased. I remember wondering if my mother, just a few feet away, had seen or heard any of this. I think I would have remembered if she had. She never commented on my developing body except to shame it, like the time she and Daddy, my sister, and I were at a shopping center. Out of the blue she turned to me and angrily whispered, "Your shorts are too tight, people can see your vulva." *What's a vulva?* She hadn't bothered to tell me the difference between vulva and vagina, but that day I knew both were bad and needed to be controlled.

Compared to my mother's reprimand, my father's squeeze was reaffirming and somehow predictive: future men would touch and comment on my breasts, especially given how breast-focused the 1950s and early '60s were. Perhaps that's why my mother focused on my nether parts, an anatomy we shared. My mother did not, could not, share my pleasure in breasts because as a child one of hers had been scarred and flattened by a Fourth of July sparkler that set afire the sleeve of her dress. Hence my mother's fear of fire: a ban on Christmas lights and candles; an electric stove, not gas; no cigarette lighters in the house, though she smoked all the time; no charcoal grill. And no nursing her three children. We all knew about her accident, and she frequently remarked to me and my sister that Daddy wasn't the kind of man who judged a woman by her bosom.

I wanted big breasts and I got 'em. I rather enjoyed when the high school boys outside of shop class mooed at me as I walked by. But I hadn't yet shared my breasts with anyone. My father's squeeze had been casual, not predatory or salacious; it didn't propel me into early sexual experimentation. And it certainly didn't have anything to do with the military strategies of young men wanting to feel me up. But during the winter of *Rubber Soul,* in the front seat of a cold car, that military analogy was right on the money.

He was a freshman at Penn State, my first older man, and he wore a Duffle coat with toggle buttons (all the rage in Liverpool), and he had a Beatles haircut. Betty and I had gone to the neighborhood rec center for a dance. I have no memory of how this boy approached me, as I wasn't used to boys doing that, but somehow we ended up in his car, Betty and Tommy in the backseat, and me and Penn State up front.

In the car it soon became clear he would feel me up. How would he do it, I wondered? Curiosity rendered me immobile, yet I was still hyperaware of every maneuver he made. What surprised me most was his military precision. Like generals in a war movie repositioning pushpins topped with colored flags across a huge map, the boy hovering over me was strategizing.

My right breast was his objective. Moving from the south (that would be my waistband), a few fingers of his left hand, tentative and cold, pat-patted my bare skin underneath my sweater. From the west, first over my shoulder, then in a sudden about-face encroaching from the side, his right hand in a new assault. Retreat, attack, retreat—it went on for minutes, all the while kissing, rubbing our faces blue. Then, three fingers from the south resumed their diagonal ascent at the same time the hand from the west boldly swooped down to meet it, trapping my breast like a fish caught in his bare hands. But the fish quickly wiggled out of his grip, and turning to the backseat I said, *Betty, time to go.* We laughed the whole way home at his short-lived victory.

And what if it had been John Lennon in that front seat? Everything I've read about him regarding girlfriends and wives suggests he was a gentle, kind, well-mannered lover. Not a battlefield, his hand on a woman's breast, but a place he might have called home. At least it's nice to imagine John as this kind of lover. But we also know he had sex with prostitutes and groupies, and mindless, drug-fueled orgies while touring. In his memoir, *The Cake and the Rain: A Memoir,* songwriter Jimmy Webb describes in detail an ugly sexual exchange between John and a woman during the so-called Lost Weekend, the eighteen months John was out of control in Los Angeles in 1973–1974. Jimmy Webb didn't have to mention that incident, but he did anyway.

Julia's death fueled John's songwriting. "I Call Your Name," recorded by the Beatles in 1964, was actually written in 1958, the year she died. Paul suggests that the name John calls out for could have been either Julia's or Alf's, but Julia's makes more sense given how soon after her death John wrote the song. In another early song, "It Won't Be Long," John sings about being "good" because a certain someone is returning home, and as the song builds in excitement at that possibility, he sings, "It won't be long till I belong to you."

Notice the pronoun shift: it's not you belong to me, the usual romantic configuration. The song "You Belong to Me" was a 1952 hit by Jo Stafford, the first record by a female artist to become number one in Britain. If John didn't hear Stafford's original, then he more than likely heard the 1962 version by the Duprees. John's reversal of who belongs to whom in "It Won't Be Long" suggests a parental as opposed to a romantic attachment. The urgency in his voice aligns more with a young boy's desperation regarding who he belongs to, his mother or his Aunt Mimi. When these Beatles songs first came out, listeners didn't know John's history, but today it's impossible to listen to them and not hear his childhood grievances, the pain of his loss registering in simple, direct lyrics.

These early songs were tentative explorations, unlike the 1968 "Julia," a lilting, almost whispered paean to John's mother. But two years later, he composes "Mother," a wet lash of a song, the product of primal scream therapy that excoriates both Julia and Alf. Whether through cries, whispers, or screams, John's psychological confusion about his mother works its way to the surface by condensing his emotional history into short, powerful songs. The rest of us have to find other ways to untangle our feelings about our parents.

I'm holding a photograph of a woman. Do I know her? In a manner of speaking, as she is my mother, approximately sixteen years before I was born. She's youthful, sunburned, and vibrant. The brim of her straw hat is as broad as her shoulders. She's wearing a sleeveless overall with two patch pockets on the chest, little Mary Jane sandals on her feet, and she's smiling big. This is my mother, a white American woman sitting on a sea wall in Veracruz, Mexico, circa 1932, my mother before my father, my brother and sister, before me, before she got sick, before her breast was dug out by Army doctors convinced the scar tissue would turn cancerous, before she looked so old and haggard that once as a teenager I refused to publicly acknowledge her as my mother.

But here she is, shiny and happy, smiling as though it's the easiest thing in the world to know her, she's that bright, that open. But when I look at this photograph, I know nothing except that she's beautiful and happy, and that knowing she's my mother makes me sad and guilty.

Does knowledge, even retroactive knowledge, confer love? If I had known my mother better, could that knowledge have created an earlier and deeper understanding of the woman who birthed me? I had her for twenty-six years, ten more than John Lennon had Julia, but I can't say for sure if she ever had me. Or wanted me. One time, in an outburst probably fueled by any number of domestic frustrations, my mother told me, "I wish I had left you in the hospital." I wonder, do all failed diaphragm babies hear this one time or another in their lives?

The Veracruz photograph is one of many from the time she spent in Mexico in the 1930s. She never hid them from us, nor was she shy about telling me and my sister about the Mexican Air Force General she was involved with, though I have no recollection of how or when in our childhood she first mentioned her Mexican lover. She had kept silver jewelry from Taxco, could rattle off Spanish curses, told us about the terror of an earthquake, of tarantulas in her riding boots and, most of all, that she had learned to fly a biplane and had a wing-shaped pin to prove it, though I'm pretty sure it was just a military pin the General had given her.

This was my "before" mother. My "after" mother didn't even drive, was frequently ill, and took a job only when the money was so low she had no choice but to work. She worked in the gift department of Woodward and Lothrop, a local department store close to our home. Once, while riding the escalator to the floor she worked on, I heard her coughing before I saw her, and when I did see her, it took some seconds for her to come into a comfortable focus. I was embarrassed by how she looked and angry that she had to be on her feet all day; but I was furious that on her break the first thing she did was light up a Camel. Compared to other saleswomen, she was poorly dressed, though always neat. When she wore her green blazer, she secured the Mexican aviator pin above the breast pocket. It became a conversation piece, and she enjoyed telling customers about flying across the Mexican sky, living an adventurous life so different from the one she was living after becoming a wife and mother. None of the customers knew she stuffed her bra with Kleenex to even things out, to add a bit of shape; but I knew this.

Then she was taken off the floor and made a clerk in the dry cleaning and fur storage department, which was located down a distant corridor. Here customers were women who carried their off-season minks like sacred vestments in the crook of their arms, who had opera gloves to be relined, expensive dresses to be cleaned and pressed. It was heavy work for my mother. I know this because a few years later I had the same job. The job's only benefit for me was that I could read at the desk when there were no customers, but I doubt if my mother ever did that, as she worked Saturdays, the busiest day.

Julia Lennon was a free spirit, maybe even a ridiculous one by English middle class standards, but she was never alone, her family never disowned her. She was the pluck on their tightly wound strings. She seemed to love life, or at least disguised any despair about it with a belying casualness. She was sexual; she liked to strut and tell jokes. Being married or becoming a mother didn't seem to change Julia. One could argue she loved her party life more than her son, but perhaps we should judge her more generously, as that son always loved her and seemed to know her in some important, fundamental way. He was never embarrassed by her, I'm sure.

The smiling woman on the seawall in Veracruz is single, not yet a wife and mother. Marriage changed her. I learned how much it can change a woman when I became a wife and mother myself. So this is the great robbery, the hole women fall into, the state-sanctioned cohabitative rhythms

and demands that declare at regular intervals one's narrow-
ing future, a readjustment of life's compass so that the needle points to *Here* and no longer *There*. Veracruz, like old
photographs, fades. But my mother kept her lover's letters,
his newspaper clippings, hotel stubs and train timetables.
Somewhere a long time ago there was a lace mantilla, but it's
gone, perhaps in one of the tug-of-wars my sister and I were
famous for.

My mother loved her children, but I'm not sure she took
delight in them. She was forty-two when I was born. There
were two toddlers already at home, and while carrying me
she developed toxemia and spent some time confined. Imagine the tiredness, the aches awakened by the requirements of
caring for three children. My father was around, perhaps my
grandmother, at least for a short while. But the roaches still
persisted, streaming down the kitchen wall only to fall into
the heating baby formula, which my mother had to throw
out and start again. The March wind caused her hands to
bleed, but the diapers were clean and sun-dried. I spent my
first three months in the bottom drawer of my parents' bedroom dresser. These are stories mothers tell their children,
their daughters especially, perhaps as warnings not to marry,
or if they do, to marry up the economic ladder. These are the
stories I heard.

My mother's name was Martha. She had a wounded
breast. I did not love her as I should have.

THINGS I HEARD TODAY

I doubt if all the peanut M&Ms in the world could entice me to listen straight through in one marathon session to all the Beatles albums while lying on my couch. Thirty inches of snow and no place to go haven't motivated me, nor has that half lid of weed I keep forgetting to smoke. How can I write about Beatles songs if I don't listen to them?

But I offer a historical precedent in Thomas DeQuincey, that delectable Englishman who confessed, "I have not been able to compose the notes for this part of my narrative into any regular and connected shape [as] I am a helpless sort of person." Tom, I can dig it: the *desire* is there; the will, not so much. But unlike DeQuincey's, my inactivity is not due to opium but to certain philosophical and historical impediments which, paradoxically, present themselves as a bounty of riches.

First off, *which* Beatles album will I listen to and in what format? The Beatles albums I bought as a teenager, though precious to me, have been irrevocably thinned by repeated play beneath substandard styluses, so listening to them won't work. Also, the spines of their cardboard sleeves were mauled by the rabbit that Animal, a stud muffin from my biker days, gave me when it was just a wee ball of fur. That wee ball became a New Zealand White—you know, the rabbits originally bred for meat, the older ones sold as roasters. Mine had nervous teeth and liked using them. Consequently, my Beatles albums, like damaged relics, have been secured out of harm's way, and I have no intention of buying duplicate ones. The rabbit went to PETA.

That leaves CDs, but again, which ones? Until 1967 with *Sgt. Pepper,* Beatles albums issued in America on Capitol differed from those originally issued in the UK on the Parlophone label. I didn't know this. Nor did I know that when CD versions of the albums first appeared, they conformed to the Parlophone ordering of tracks. Consequently, the first time I listened to my *Rubber Soul* CD and heard "Drive My Car" instead of "I've Just Seen a Face," the anticipated aural *deja vu* embedded in my teenage brain was severely scrambled. Before my friend Allen cut me a bootleg CD of Capitol's *Rubber Soul,* I couldn't thrill to the acoustic thrust of "I've Just Seen a Face" being immediately dismantled by the alien swerve of the sitar on the next song, "Norwegian Wood." That is, not unless I got off the couch and opened the LP vault, which I seemed helpless to do.

We know the song is not the record, but what if the record isn't the record? Now that Capitol has issued its Beatles albums as CDs, this conundrum only deepens.

Sequence also gets embedded into memory and affects how we hear an entire album because a CD plays both sides of an album without interruption, another incentive to lie on the couch. As a continuous sequence, the songs on an album can approach the aesthetic standard of poetry, *The best words in the best order,* as Samuel Taylor Coleridge defines it. Imagine if Capitol had cut a different version of *Sgt. Pepper?* It's bad enough to learn that of the songs chosen for the album, "A Day in The Life" was the first song *recorded* during the *Pepper* sessions and not the culmination of the songs that precede it on the album. But it's impossible to conceive of the album ending with any other song. Records, like poems, are *made* things, and sequencing emphasizes this fact.

Then there's the matter of History/history and the distinctions between them. For example, as a teenager I thought that girls in Liverpool listened to the same Beatles albums as I did, but, because the US albums were different from the UK ones, they didn't. Allowing for these differences in one's listening experience is an example of how little-h histories can dilute the universalizing impact of capital-H History. Because not everyone hears the same album, little-h histories tend to destabilize the artifact. What is the "correct" album is now up for grabs.

The excellent detailed examinations of the Beatles' recording sessions by Ian MacDonald and Mark Lewisohn further complicate both types of history. After learning that Paul played the scorching guitar solo on George Harrison's "Taxman," I had to reconsider what I previously thought about George as lead guitarist, a little-h history irritation, and how the group as a whole supposedly worked, a capital-H History, as one assumes lead guitar means every guitar solo is George's. Now that I know otherwise, this fact both disrupts and expands how I listen to "Taxman" and to the Beatles in general.

The more I learn about capital-H Beatles history, the more I want to investigate where it intersects with my own history. At what point does factual knowledge interfere with my listening pleasure? Am I adjusting my responses to the songs in order to prove to my audience that I'm knowledgeable about Beatles recordings? Will my gathering of factual knowledge eclipse that fanatical teenage girl, that original *me* who circled in pencil the titles of her favorite two songs on

Meet the Beatles, their first Capitol album, and twenty-three months later, older and much more sophisticated, scribbled across the back of *Rubber Soul* in a cramped high school cursive this line of poetry: *Through the crystal glazed paine [sic] I stare.*

She, and millions more like her, should not be overlooked or forgotten, as it was her/their responses that made the Beatles a worldwide phenomenon. Beatlemania, more so than the band, was the initial big story, one predictably absorbed into capital-H History. But the band's records impacted many more little-h histories, ones not reified by a photograph or edited into a news clip.

It should surprise no one that the big books that tackle the actual recordings and their histories were written by men, the gender that couldn't participate in Beatlemania except as waiting courtiers to fainting sisters and girlfriends. Instead, these boys-to-men hunkered down with the records, and later with the tapes and the entire Abbey Road archive. To accomplish what Ian MacDonald and Mark Lewisohn have done goes beyond a forensic investigation of the Beatles' variorum; it is a kind of controlled hysteria of the mind: to collect, discern, and establish a capital-H account while immersed in one of the most private little-h endeavors of the modern world: listening to a record . . . over and over again.

MacDonald and Lewisohn got up off of their respective couches and produced definitive but divergent critical scholarship. I enjoy being helpless before this fact. All I have to do is listen and absorb whatever I'm hearing at the moment and see where it leads me. I can let the knowledge of a particular song penetrate me, or I can simply groove on its bass line. Nothing to prove, nothing to settle, nothing to get hung about: just me and 212 songs (let's not argue about *that,* OK?) I may or may not listen to. In no particular order. Here goes.

SIDE ONE, 1964–1965

The Beatles' Second Album
(CD of Capitol's second 1964 US release)

Stupid title, but their most rocking album. Lots of forward thrust, downshifting for the slower numbers, reaching maximum tension and acceleration with "Money," "Long Tall Sally," and "She Loves You." Six covers and five Lennon-McCartneys. John's voice dominates, but Paul's rendition of Little Richard's "Long Tall Sally" makes you want to run through your house buck naked.

George leads off with Chuck Berry's "Roll Over, Beethoven," just as he did at the Beatles' first US concert at the Washington, DC Coliseum, February 11, 1964. On that night, George's guitar didn't pick up until he plugged it into another amp, and then he was out of tune, but the song is not the record, and on the record he's just super. On the UK albums, George didn't gain the opening cut until 1966 with his "Taxman" on *Revolver,* though some might argue that his G-eleventh suspended fourth chord that opens *A Hard Day's Night* deserves that honor. Either way, the torch has been passed: Beethoven, Berry, Beatles.

The sound is white, though the cover songs were originally done by black singers and groups. But with their glottal tug, curled r's, and a rawness that combined beautiful and often angular harmonies, the Beatles' voices are Other—street-wise English tempered by church singing. No one in America sounded like this, not even such singular singers as Dell Shannon, Lew Christy, or Roy Orbison.

Except for Ringo, none of the four danced, so no smooth moves with hands and feet like American black groups. The songs on this album stab instead of glide; they pound instead of bop—just listen to the drums on "Thank You Girl." With these songs, it's not so much the hip-rolling emphasis of

R & B as it is discovering new ways of letting rhythm take over your entire body, inviting you to feel free and break out as opposed to the elegant precision of black dance styles. "Money" is the example many point to. John ravishes it, shreds it, and closes with such finality you'd hand over your bank account to him. There's an urgency to the song, every word almost chopped off, a conviction missing in Barrett Strong's original version, in part because the backup voices responding to Strong's demands are female whereas Paul and George's backup reinforces John's demands. This male solidarity conveys the grossness of John's need, and within that need is a threat the listener is compelled to respond to: *give me money.*

I'd grown up with movies and television, the radio and rock and roll, but there was no precedent in my life for the sound the Beatles made, even when they sang songs I was familiar with. 1964 was the first time I sensed that I was part of a sweeping historical change, and I was helpless against it.

Beatles for Sale
(UK album Dec. 1964 / *Beatles '65,* US Dec. 1964)

On "No Reply," John's voice and the driving 12-string guitars plow this song into the common ground of human neediness, the fertile dramas of love and betrayal, whether those of a stalker boyfriend or of Greek myths. John sings so fraughtfully we're wise not to push him on the details, because they may reveal some ancient fault line we're in no hurry to see crack open.

Singing like this exposes a man's emotional intricacies, which has always been one quality of rock and roll songs, be they about heart-wrenching pain or raucous joy. But some highly emotional love songs like Elvis's "Heartbreak Hotel" or Roy Orbison's "Crying," because of their hyperbolic singing style, invite parodies that can diminish their lyrics. "No

Reply" is sung straight as it moves matter-of-factly through three distinct emotional phases: factual disbelief at seeing his girl with someone else, bodily reaction of feeling he could die, and a bargaining threat in the hopes of regaining her.

As a sixteen-year-old girl, I was intrigued by the hurt in John's voice rather than by any threat he may have been expressing. Two years earlier I had cried in the girls' bathroom of my junior high after slow dancing with Buzzy to "A Million to One," a one-hit wonder by Jimmy Charles. Hadn't all girls done that type of crying, a typical teenage Friday night weep? John's pain, however, felt adult, more substantial, the qualities in his voice transcending the sidewalk specifics of the song's storyline to become a song *about* pain, pain as old as tragedy or as current as being unfriended on Facebook.

"I'll Be Back" is "a melodic essay in major/minor uncertainty mirrored in the emotional instability of its lyric." Though here Ian MacDonald is writing about "I'll Be Back," he could just as well be weighing in on T. S. Eliot's "The Love Song of J. Alfred Prufrock." Both the song and the poem entered my life within a three-week span between December 15, 1964, when Capitol's *Beatles '65* went on sale, and January 4, 1965, the day Eliot died. I knew nothing about Eliot until Mr. Diggs, my high school English teacher, recited "Prufrock" from memory to the class. Before hearing "Prufrock," I had wanted to be a hairstylist, like Maureen Starkey, Ringo's first wife. But after hearing the poem, I put my teasing comb away for good. I now wanted to be a poet.

Learning about Eliot taught me the value and habit of language, how to analyze it, how to measure it, how to turn it into poetry. It also solidified the importance of mystery. "I'll Be Back" is one of John's most mysterious songs, but unlike in his later language-driven creations such as "I Am the Walrus," the song's subject, a romantic breakup, is par for popular music. However, the song's musical structure, its inseparable harmony and melody, the foreboding 12-string strumming, and John's plaintive voice create something never before heard and that the Beatles never repeated, though the haunting quality of the *White Album's* "Dear Prudence" comes close.

In 2014, I bought the *Beatles '65* CD because I wanted to hear "I'll Be Back" as I had originally heard it on the US album, tucked between "Honey Don't" and "She's a Woman." I paid for the CD with my credit card, but in 1965 I gleefully stole the *Collected Poems of T. S. Eliot* from my high school library. I still have the book, its pages festooned with penciled comments, the scalloped links I drew down the page marking "Prufrock's" rhyme scheme, and many underlined phrases full of what I thought, and rightly so, were sexual innuendos. Mr. Diggs's recitation directed my ear away from poems with lines like "Listen my children and you shall hear" to denser, more melodic ones such as "the evening spread out against the sky / like a patient etherized upon a table." I leapt into that figurative mystery and looked for it in everything I heard, read, or saw. And, because "Prufrock" also mentions "the yellow fog . . . soot that falls from chimneys . . . toast and tea," it was easy to imagine Liverpool and London, places for which I had already created a private geography, one I hoped to test one day against the real thing.

Beatles for Sale, like its predecessor *A Hard Day's Night,* is an album that declares the Beatles' artistic intentions. Forthwith, they would experiment with various sound effects, complicate their songs' structures and melodies, investigate mature and often arcane themes, even engage in sophisticated satire, and they would cultivate the ability to create an album as a complete, stand-alone work of art.

In 1965, I was also inspired to begin my own artistic creations—by a learned and elegantly dressed black man who recited "The Love Song of J. Alfred Prufrock" before a room full of stunned suburban white teenagers. Thank you, Paul L. Diggs.

Rubber Soul (Capitol issue, Dec. 6, 1965)

When *Rubber Soul* arrived, I simply absorbed it as my daily meal; its beautiful and provocative music became an essential nutrient in my life. Earlier songs like "Things We Said Today" and "I'll Be Back" prepared me for this new album, but other influences were also at work. Since I had declared myself a poet, a life without art had become impossible; I didn't cultivate a new personality so much as a new way of being a person. *Rubber Soul* seemed to fit with that new person. Was this the time I began to iron my hair? Probably. Did I begin to buy books for my "library"? Yes, and I also began collecting albums, all kinds. My circle of friends began to change as its outer curves filled with guitarists and long-striding girls who didn't feverishly wait for the September issue of *Seventeen.* Buzzy had been "sent up" to reform school shortly after the tearful dance I had with him in ninth grade. Now it was awkward, stuttering Jewish boys, good at math and never been kissed. With their shirttails half out and their skinny arms, I viewed them as artists. They might not have combed their hair, but they played Martin guitars.

When I was a high school senior, my future loomed. College? Work? A cold water flat in New York City where I would dedicate myself to writing? I couldn't afford the first, and the last was a cartoon version of a Platonic ideal. That left work, which was fine, because a paycheck meant more money for books and records.

I approached *Rubber Soul* with a religious intensity. But to my older sister Marlene, the album was just great fun, full of songs we could sing and harmonize with. One favorite was "You Won't See Me" with its "u-la-la-la" as background to the melody. We switched harmonies between these songs, not always successfully because the Beatles had three harmonizing singers and we were only two.

Sometimes a song's small detail or instrumental passage caught Marlene's attention in strange ways, such as when she would bang on the bathroom door while singing *ba-ba-ba-ba-baba*, the fuzz bass part on "Think for Yourself." It was a duet for voice and fist, a reminder that we had only one toilet for the five of us.

Worse was our ripping off John's famous sniffing sound on "Girl." Whenever one of us lifted an arm, the other came nosing about with "Ah, girl, girl, sniffffffffff," which we thought was hysterical. John's sniff was bluer than ours, a naughty nod to his 1961 excursion to Paris's Left Bank, or perhaps to Liverpool's notorious lack of indoor plumbing. We, however, were just sisters enjoying being unladylike.

When Marlene and I were younger, we used to sit on our bed facing each other and try not to cry while singing the verses of "Flow Gently Sweet Afton." We never succeeded, and the tears soon gave way to giggles and tightly crossed legs. But we were dead serious when we performed "Silent Night" at Christmas. Tucked away a few steps up the staircase, we waited for our invisible father's countdown. I sang melody and Marlene broke in with a descant. We had to sing loud enough so our family sitting around the dining room table could hear us, and we generally succeeded, but not without some wiggling and pinching on the dark stairs.

In 1966, Marlene was working in an office and still living at home, but I saw her as a worldly woman. She played piano, could sight-read and sing a capella, draw when she felt the urge, and sewed many cocktail dresses to wear on dates with her Greek-American boyfriend, Jimmy, he of the red MG convertible and exotic ancestry. With her golden hair piled high and a pair of stilettos holding up her long-waisted athletic body, Marlene was glamorous, mature and, unbeknownst to me, deeply unhappy. She once said of "Norwegian Wood," *It is very weird, you know that, don't you?* But of course I didn't; I just thought it was poetic. I think she was hinting something about her life, but I was reluctant to inquire, and she was always secretive.

Jimmy was more exotic than Marlene's earlier boyfriend, Gratton, a quasi beatnik my mother once refused to allow in the house because he had grown a beard. I witnessed this moment of maternal idiocy while Marlene was upstairs getting ready, and, taking pity on Gratton, I went outside and stood with him on the front walk, where we debated whether folk music was or wasn't better than rock and roll. And I made sure to tell him I liked his beard.

Jimmy was into folk music, too, but what he really loved was Peter Sellers movies and James Bond. This rubbed off on Marlene, and for a while she loved all things British. She taught me what a pun was; what car parts the British words "bonnet" and "boot" applied to, which we thought was hilarious given our love of clothing and shoes. She could do voices just like Sellers, and she excelled in imitating Margaret Rutherford, too. After attending a folk concert, she began to sing ballads, usually the high-lonesome ones that Jean Ritchie sang.

Marlene always thought the Beatles were boys as opposed to men, though she was taken by the photograph of George in cowboy regalia on the back of *Rubber Soul,* perhaps because she was heading toward cowboy land herself. Almost overnight she was done with Jimmy and his red MG. Now it was horse trainers, farmers, American men with creased faces and callused hands who didn't know Peter Sellers from Jim Beam. She went from George Harrison to George Jones, replacing her young Greek cineaste with a World War Two vet who chewed tobacco.

In more than one way, I lost my sister to country and western music, and it took me years to hear in those honkeytonk songs and sad ballads what she had heard at nineteen. Though singing the harmonies of *Rubber Soul* with Marlene brought us together, it also marked our departure. *Rubber Soul* was just the beginning of our departure; at sixteen, I was becoming a snob.

SIDE TWO, 1966–1970

Yesterday . . . and Today; Revolver

Capitol's ninth Beatles album, *Yesterday . . . and Today*, arrived on June 20, 1966, a few days after I graduated from high school. Capitol's version of *Revolver* arrived on August 8. In the forty-one intervening days, Richard Speck was arrested for murdering eight student nurses in Chicago, and Charles Whitman climbed the tower on the campus of the University of Texas and opened fire, killing sixteen. The world was getting hairy, and all of 1966 would turn out to be one long rite of passage for me, for the Beatles and for America.

Yesterday . . . and Today was a hodgepodge of an album, delivering four songs initially on the UK *Rubber Soul,* two from the UK *Help!* and three from the upcoming UK *Revolver.* But American listeners didn't know this. My two favorites from *Yesterday . . . and Today* were "Drive My Car" and "And Your Bird Can Sing." The real pull of this album is its notorious "butcher" cover, the initial photograph of the Beatles dressed in white coats and holding bloody doll parts and slabs of meat. Horrified by the response some had to this cover, Capitol pulled the albums and replaced them with a new cover, though a number of suppliers simply pasted the new photo over the old and put the albums back in the stores. My album cover, a bloodless photo, shows the Beatles benignly posed amid steamer trunks, but Alan Livingston, then president of Capitol, foreseeing a collectible, kept a private stash of the original albums with their bloody cover. Paul and John are on record saying that the bloody photograph represented the horrors of Vietnam. In 2006, one of Livingston's sealed albums with the original photo sold for $39,000.

And Richard Speck and Charles Whitman? They were the warm-up act for Charles Manson three years later in 1969.

Every day that summer, my best friend Betty and I read the papers, trying to get our heads around the Speck murders. How could eight women not fight off one skinny man? Eight men certainly could. Despite imagining being the nurse who escaped death by hiding under a bed, our inability to answer that question manifested itself as an ugly reality: all women, one way or another, are marked. Quietly, our bodies had begun teaching us that all women might be potential victims. Self-interest and carnage—that was 1966.

I had a new friend, Rita, an iconoclastic, abrasive, razor-sharp Jew who saw something edgy and worthwhile in me and staked her claim by insisting she sit next to me in glee club. With Rita I explored DC, visiting the Saville book-store in Georgetown where she'd lounge in a stairwell reading Camus in French while I tried to look like I could read French, too. I don't remember when I began listening to Bob Dylan, but Rita leant me his first, eponymous album. Later, in his wickedly portentous "The Ballad of the Thin Man," Dylan updated Eliot's timid Prufrock with his own Mr. Jones, and I immediately switched allegiance for Tom over to Bob. Dylan was immensely more alluring with his curly hair, polka dot shirt, and wild riffs than owl-eyed Eliot. Now, certain songs were as important to me as were certain poems.

No one singer or group dislodged my loyalty to the Beatles, but *Revolver* was a distinct demarcation between, or perhaps an embarkation toward, a wider musical appreciation. By 1966 I was deep into country and electric blues, researching roots music for school projects and self-satisfaction. To make room on my shelves for Paul Oliver's groundbreaking *Blues Fell This Morning* (later retitled *The Meaning of the Blues*) and other books, I tossed the piles of Beatles paraphernalia I'd accumulated since 1964. Did I really need all those *Sixteen* magazines with their two-inch snaps and fatuous captions? Hadn't I advanced past the swooning stage and accumulation of trivia concerning the Fab Four? There was simply too much good music around to limit my love. The Rolling Stones, the Animals, Wayne Fontana and the Mindbenders, Manfred Mann, the Kinks, the Zombies— these groups had my attention from the beginning, but now there was Cream, Them, the Mothers of Invention, and Leonard Cohen. I had also begun listening to classical music, especially Rachmaninoff, and one afternoon I listened to all of Mahler's *Resurrection Symphony* while lying on the floor, something I'd never do today.

Considering how sophisticated I was becoming, you'd think I would have appreciated the musical and technical advancements of *Revolver,* but I didn't. "Tomorrow Never Knows" slid right pass me, registering as comical, if it registered at all. Though Rita, and even Betty, had expressed an interest in taking LSD, all drugs scared me, especially ones that could potentially make you feel like you were dying.

John Lennon could sing "Turn off your mind, relax and float downstream / It is not dying . . ." all he wanted, the tab dissolving in his lovely mouth, but upstairs in a messy bedroom my mother really was dying, coughing her life away, surrounded by stiff, bloodied Kleenex that reminded me of circling sharks. She had missed my high school graduation, and she would miss the upcoming Christmas, which would not be the first she had spent in hospital. I couldn't hear what John was saying because the last thing I wanted was to turn off my mind, given how active it was becoming. Unlike some, I didn't want to take a trip just to see what it was like; I wanted to live and be safe in the small world I was used to.

Perhaps my investigations into the blues had inoculated me against everything but reality—sex, grief, and hard work were the blue's inescapable subjects. As an attitude toward life, "cut you if you stand, shoot you if you run" suited my view of life better than floating downstream; it certainly fed my need for drama. I doubted, too, if "Tomorrow Never Knows" could prepare me for sex, whereas I theoretically learned a lot from the blues, though it would be two years before I would deploy this knowledge in any meaningful way, and then with less than spectacular results.

Now, of course, I know the value of *Revolver* and the technical and musical advancements of Lennon's song. However, I'm still defensive when Ian MacDonald writes that it "challenges not only seven centuries of Western music, but the operating premise of Western civilization itself. When Lennon's voice rises out of the seething dazzle of churning [tape] loops . . . the first words he utters, 'Turn off your mind,' are a mystical negation of all progressive intellectual enterprise." Trouble is, in 1966 I wanted to be a progressive intellectual enterprise. Or at least try. I was just seventeen, you know what I mean?

Sgt. Pepper's Lonely Hearts Club Band

By June 1967, when *Sgt. Pepper* was released, I was learning to swoon more intellectually, but first I had to help my father get up off the floor. It wasn't unusual to find him there, listening or, after a day of writing, groaning to music. When we kids were younger and lighter, we'd walk up and down his back, which seemed to offset the pain that had settled there from hours hunched over his desk. When he wrote or arranged music, he used simple tools: no. 1 Venus pencils, a fat ink pen with a stylus he'd shave periodically with a small blade, a gum eraser, and blotting paper. First he'd write in pencil, erase, correct, and then do it all again in black ink. From time to time, he'd leave his desk and go to the piano in the living room and bang out a few chords. Often he wrote late at night, and what banging he did then didn't wake us so much as register a reassurance that, like a clock chiming the hours, progress was being made. In the morning he'd sleep, a beached whale, and not appear until noon.

Sgt. Pepper was not the first Beatles effort to be lauded by the establishment press, but it was the one that solidified their reputation as serious and culturally important musicians. Yet when I listen to it today I have mixed feelings, as it seems both a step up and away from previous recordings. *Sgt. Pepper* is supposedly their "concept album," a status concomitantly vague and edifying, and one with risks, especially if artifice overruns spontaneity, which is the case with this album. The concept was Paul's. Now that the band had stopped touring, they could reproduce a "live" concert on record, not as the Beatles but as Sgt. Pepper's Lonely Hearts Club Band, a Northern band with Victorian themes and costumes. I loved the album and knew it was important because, except for the title cut, its songs didn't invite you to dance but to listen. I gave it my full attention. My reading of T. S. Eliot helped with that. I had advanced to "The Waste Land" and was trying to understand how the individual sections of a long poem related to the whole. When I listened to *Sgt. Pepper,* I struggled to decipher its themes in order to get at its "concept." As *Pepper* was the first album to include its lyrics on its sleeve, listening also involved reading the album, which made my investigation easier but also more imperative: *What did it all mean?*

Lying on the floor with my father listening to *Sgt. Pepper* was the opposite of conceptual, and he cared nothing about any possible themes; he was after the music, and any lyrics that might particularly strike him were extra.

So, what did Daddy like on *Sgt. Pepper?* John's "Good Morning Good Morning," because of the chickens, horses, barking dogs, and its bouncy insistency. Given that my father hated the Ohio farm he grew up on, fleeing at eighteen to Chicago with his trombone to begin his jazz career, I thought his choice strange. But childhood sounds run deep; perhaps he missed the animals.

His reaction to "A Day in the Life" was quite different: thoughtful listening and a congratulatory nod: "Not bad," he said, "not bad." These four words thrilled me, so I blurted out, "It's like Mahler, don't you think," but Daddy just gave me one of his looks. The song's stunning final chord, struck by three pianos and tracked four times, might have sounded like Mahler to me, but to my father it could have been the chord he banged on our piano last Wednesday at 1 a.m.

The last time I saw my father lying on the floor listening to records, he was in the den stoned on pot, grooving to Steely Dan's "Bodhisattva" playing through the headphones. It must have been 1975. My mother had died, and my sister had left home, as had my brother. I completely understood what Daddy was doing, as music has a power over us, and he was feeling it. Like the daughter in "She's Leaving Home," my father was ready for some fun. Widowed, too-long absent from the music he used to play, and perhaps nostalgic for a bit of smoke, he would soon move back to Ohio, back to where he was born. He would marry two more times and spend his remaining fifteen years writing music.

Tim Riley lambastes Lennon's "I Am the Walrus," the best cut on 1967's *Magical Mystery Tour,* by calling it a "mock cryptic," one that "bears no relation to a fixed viewpoint." Well, hello, Modernism!—and Postmodernism and the Language Poetry movement, too, all of which Lennon was ignorant of, and it seems Tim Riley is as well. With its crosshatching of references, languages, historical timeframes, and allusions, Modernism awakened the arts after the First World War. Learning about it awakened me, too.

1967 to 1970 were my years of the "isms": empiricism, socialism, imperialism, solipsism, sexism. I was working nights but attended junior college during the day, learning what would matter most to me throughout my life: how to read, how to understand history, and, most important, how to argue. Though bold in many of my classes and in my writing, I wasn't a stellar student so much as an excited one. Fortunately, I had many teachers who approved of my excitement.

Because I was shy and fearful, I remained on the periphery of certain social circles, and my advances into the counterculture were quaint: my sister made me a full-length burnt-orange velvet skirt that I wore when I went into Georgetown with my friends. I had a gay friend and we went to gay bars; we visited all-night diners. I tried my best to enjoy the unfurnished apartments my acquaintances rented—mattresses on the floor, roaches in the kitchen, and one time a human turd on the outdoor stoop—but I didn't want to live in any of them. I began having sex; I became an artist's model and had a brief affair with my philosophy professor, a man who took Polaroids of me while reading aloud the advice column in *Screw.* I made him tear up the photos, and we soon parted. In the school cafeteria, a classmate arguing with me about Schopenhauer suddenly yelled, "I'd never marry a woman like you, I'd never marry you." I didn't even know his name. The first time I smoked grass was in the attic bedroom of a high school kid I had a crush on. In case we had sex, I had brought along a piece of Saran Wrap, an amateur's prophylactic. I didn't need it. He was a heavy stoner, and as I lay transfixed by the horse-and-cowboy pattern of the wallpaper above his bed he asked, "You like that feeling? If you do, I can get you some acid 'cos it's like 200 times more than what you're feeling now." Clearly, I was in over my head.

A member of the Jefferson Airplane pirouetted through campus wearing a black cloak. A boy I liked was going to Paris to meet friends on Bastille Day; he had purchased a suede fringed coat for the journey. Snarly Vietnam vets in camouflage jackets suddenly appeared on campus. They seemed older, slouching in the cafeteria or huddling on the sidewalk, cupping cigarettes in their fists. I once watched one of them, a friend of my future husband, tie off his arm and shoot up with red wine. I felt so aghast at this all I wanted to do was go home, sit on the couch next to my mother, and watch Johnny Carson. I believe that my having to work and live at home kept me from many of the excesses my peers avidly pursued. That and my own fears.

But I was awakened as well. 1967 to 1970 were my awakening years, a true shock of the new that channeled my energies toward deeper engagements with literature and creative writing. After *Magical Mystery Tour,* the Beatles began to recede in my priorities. "A Whiter Shade of Pale" and Leonard Cohen's songs held my attention more than "All You Need Is Love" or "I Am the Walrus." Cohen's songs especially were brimming with sexual intrigue and powerful lusts and transcended the *Playboy* mentality common in the US.

Ideas, and new writers, excited me. I had a wonderful teacher who tutored me in contemporary poetry and turned me on to Hemingway, Theodore Roethke, and Anne Sexton, a holy trinity of stylistic perfection, deep mystery, and the woes of being female. I wanted to combine the three in my own poetry. Another teacher told me to read James Joyce and Yeats aloud. I had an independent study in the history of ideas and became enthralled by such concepts as the Great Chain of Being and lost sleep trying to understand ambiguity, let alone why there were seven types. Would I become a scholar? I adored Ezra Pound. Would I begin to eat tulips? The entire world seemed mine if only I could read faster, think deeply, create better.

All the time I was learning about literature and criticism, I never once applied their values or tenets to any Beatles songs. Back then, few did. Today I'd have no trouble arguing that the wordplay, rhyming, alliteration, and enjambment of "I Am the Walrus" are as fascinating and as skillfully poetic as Eliot's. Or that the song's origin—John's discovery that his lyrics were being analyzed in classes at his old school, something he found laughable but which also triggered memories of playground nonsense songs—is as significant as the origin of "The Waste Land," namely, Eliot's breakdown and marital strain as opposed to the collapse of Western civilization. Though Eliot dismissed his famous poem as "just a piece of rhythmical grumbling" and Lennon, alluding to Bob Dylan's surreal lyrics, once quipped, "I can write this crap, too," "Walrus" and "The Waste Land" are creative masterpieces.

The collapsing of aesthetic differences between classic and popular art forms is a product of Postmodernism. Today, discussing Eliot and Lennon in tandem would be considered de rigueur. But before I understood Postmodernism, I had to understand Modernism. Little did I know that what I learned in junior college was training me to be a critic. For what is a lover if not a critic? The critic loves *because*. And sometimes the critic loves *although*. I would soon understand that this applies to life as well as to poetry and music.

As I really would like to get up off this couch, I'll get right to the point: 1968 to 1970 was also about SEX, my having it and John rediscovering it with Yoko Ono, his future and second wife. On the *White Album, Abbey Road,* and *Let It Be,* John sings about sex and desire and the fear that arises from both: "Happiness Is a Warm Gun," "Come Together," "I Want You (She's So Heavy)," and "Don't Let Me Down," all rockers, all "heavy" in sound, and in the case of "Come Together" full of frolicking wordplay that mirrors the freaky mess the late '60s had become. Postpsychedelic Beatles got back into the groove, and though they had been imploding for some time and finally broke apart in 1970, the band could still make great music.

It's sad to think about the end of the '60s, the end of the Beatles. In 1969, Charles Manson did his interpretive damage to the group by claiming he understood their supposedly coded lyrics and, consequently, started killing folks. That same year, a man was stabbed to death at Altamont raceway during a Stones concert. Woodstock, by all accounts, was great, but now it's become a franchise. We landed on the moon.

1970 had Kent State, Cambodia, Elvis at the White House, the Concorde's first flight, Earth Day, the deaths of Jimi Hendrix and Janis Joplin, and styles of clothing that made me look ridiculous. Did I still listen to *Abbey Road?*

Did I rush out to buy *Let It Be?* Did I lie on the floor wearing headphones, lost to all around me? No, no, no: I was pregnant and, just like the scratching of the needle signaling that the record is over, I knew that more than the Beatles had come to an end.

In the Broadway musical *Seven Lively Arts,* Ben Hecht wrote, "Old songs are more than tunes. They are little houses in which our hearts once lived." This is a lovely description of the power songs have. By 1973, my little house would explode, but I've been able to rebuild it, song by song.

OF BALLS AND THE
BEATLES

Balls. The word that Betty and I used to designate the mysterious mélange males carry between their legs, a package we
had no direct knowledge about when we were thirteen. But
what we did have was a code, a syllabic appraisal we'd sing
out to each other whenever a guy came into view: *bbbbb*. If
a man walked by in tight pants or sat in a certain way so that
something down there suggested itself through his clothing,
we'd respond *mezzoforte bbbbbbBBB*. The British slang for
this pubertal excess is "basket shopping," and we kept our
eyes out for sales. We were devoted voyeurs.

Yes, it was silly, and that's part of why we did it. I don't
remember having any overt discussion with Betty about eye-
stalking men's equipment; we colluded instinctively. Repelled
by seventh-grade hygiene films, confused by the crude drawings in slam books, and hindered by the ubiquitous business
suit, whose design signaled white-collar status but neutral-
ized any evidence of phallic individuality, we hunted for signs
of visual sexual difference in the only place two respectable
teenage girls could hangout: the shopping mall. Seated on
hard plastic chairs scattered along the mall's promenade,

Betty would look one way and I another. Whenever a man approached, if he was worthy of our assessment, we'd begin with the *bbb*s. Because we were seated waist-high to our subjects, we could peruse unimpeded. If we giggled, which happened a lot, anyone noticing us would see two silly teenage girls, not the eye-stalking perverts we really were.

Michael Landon, who played Little Joe in *Bonanza,* that sexy drama airing on Sunday evenings in the early '60s, put an end to our mall ball watching. In the comfort and privacy of Betty's paneled rec room, we turned our female gaze upon Little Joe's lovely package. No business suit for this Cartwright male. Instead, he wore light-colored, stretch-like pants and a low-slung belt that directed the eye crotchward, and because he was a bit bowlegged, his pelvis tended up. No doubt about it, he was packing. If other actors in Westerns also were, they never caught our eye. Little Joe was enough.

Betty was so taken with Little Joe that she created a Little Joe comic strip whose theme was based on a ditty we liked to sing: *Tra ra ra boom dee ay / Did you get yours today? / I got mine yesterday / that's why I walk this way.* The illustrations we created were of an increasingly bowlegged and heavy-balled Joe swaggering around town after visiting the local brothel. Eventually his *bbb*s reached the ground from overuse. Obviously we had displaced our fear of maleness onto Joe's body, making his ever-enlarging package bear the weight of our ignorance. It's impossible to know how Betty and I at thirteen would have responded to photographs of Led Zeppelin's Roger Plant singing on stage in tight pants. Poor Andy Gibb done up in split-crotch pink pants would have undone us, I'm sure.

Along with great music, the British Invasion brought great balls, ones often split across a tight seam that allowed no room for sway. The Beatles didn't dress this way, though in the group's photo on the back of *Meet the Beatles,* there's a bulge in John Lennon's slacks that I eyed at fifteen.

Like my Beatles magazines, slam books, and accordion wallets containing photographs that unfolded in a plastic waterfall, the Little Joe comic strip is gone. Between the silliness of seventh grade and high school, Betty and I normalized, or at least I think we did. We no longer stalked the *bbb*s, because by high school the male body, no longer theoretical, had become tangible through dancing, kissing, and petting. Though rare, every time a boy kissed me, I knew I was gathering helpful bodily information. And though I was horrified by the photo of a naked man Betty had shown me when I was fourteen—my first penis!—my curiosity about male anatomy only deepened. I became obsessed with boys, how they walked and gestured, their mouths, and the way their pants hung on their bodies. Surprising bolts of lust charged through me whenever I turned the pages in my high school yearbook.

But the man who really convinced me of the mystery of male sexual power was my first boss, the baker. I was sixteen. He dressed all in white, and his belly hung over his belt. In winter his undershirt was short-sleeved; in summer he wore a wife-beater. Wearing a white hat shaped like a paper boat pushed back on his thinning hair, he epitomized the working-class man, a figure out of a 1950s war movie— think Aldo Ray—who conveyed his masculinity through his ability to "do the job." I never paid attention to him until one cold evening when he asked how I was. "I'm a little chilly," I answered, and he replied "Don't worry, I'll keep you warm." Ka-boom!!!!—my uterus did a flip. All he said was six words, but I had become a woman. I was so knocked out by this experience I wrote a story about it, but when I read it to Betty she laughed because I described his belly as "protruding." I understood her criticism: in high school big bellies were laughable, something only old men had, and the opposite of sexy. But my own response to my boss's comments revealed that sexual excitation couldn't be standardized, and that what a man said, and how he said it, had its own allure.

It was about this time, too, that I realized literature could convey erotic guidance and plunged into the works of D. H. Lawrence, because in an interview Paul McCartney had mentioned reading *Lady Chatterley's Lover*. I read the banned novel, or at least the "good" parts, but Lawrence's short story "Tickets, Please" made a bigger impression, as the conflict between the main characters exposed the complications of sexual attraction through powerful, even violent scenes that gave me a new way of thinking about men. It occurred to me that men I disliked could still be sexually alluring. Or maybe that there were styles of men, and like shoes, some fit you better than others. Or that some could force you to buy a pair of shoes you never would have bought yourself. I even had a fleeting thought, brought on by watching Gary Cooper woo Suzy Parker in *Ten North Frederick Street*, that a friend's dad might be sexually attractive. But in eleventh grade, I had yet to test any of these hypotheticals.

I don't remember feeling overt lust for John Lennon; instead, I absorbed him as a totality. I didn't see John solely as a body, as I did Little Joe, because John and the Beatles had inserted talent and intelligence into the mix. John didn't have sixteen-inch biceps like Buzzy, my ninth-grade crush, but he was smart and funny. In future years I would re-appreciate men with biceps who could do all the manly things like fix the roof, but in the '60s I loved John's face, his hair, his voice, all his English differences. Most of all, I loved the existential fact of him.

Since I concentrated on him whenever I watched the Beatles perform, I must have been aware of his body's posture, the wide-legged stance he took at the microphone, what many observers viewed as an invitation to oral sex. But I knew nothing about that. Lack of sexual experience muted my response in specific ways but heightened the overall effect Lennon had on me: I wanted ALL of him, and for general purposes. This responsive "all-ness" foreshadowed future inclinations by triggering capacities in me I was just beginning to recognize but hadn't yet tested on men. And along with these capacities came distinctions: I was aware of the lump in Mick Jagger's trousers and approved of how he sang the blues, but I did not desire him. Same with Eric Burden of the Animals, who surpassed Jagger as a blues singer. These men conveyed sexy subjects, were themselves sexy, but not to me. Only Dylan affected me sexually; he could sing the blues, and he had that skinny Jewish guy thing going for him. When he sang "Baby, let me follow you down," I fantasized all kinds of things. But I did not love him as the total package; only John was that.

Part of John's allure was the clothing he wore. Brian Epstein insisted that the Beatles get out of their leathers and into designer suits, but they insisted on keeping the Cuban heeled boots that gave them a sexy, foreign vibe that others soon copied. I added these boots to the list of distinctions I was developing about men. In the 1960s, sartorial categories as stringent as medieval guilds' had developed. Greasers dressed differently from heads, hippie dudes wore sandals, and the returning vets seemed wedded to their dubbed combat boots despite what else they wore. Cowboy boots, disco and glam rock boots—men's shoes and clothing were changing, and so were the men who wore them. I took notice.

Even during their most flamboyant psychedelic years, all the Beatles looked good in what they wore. Though there's a long and honorable tradition of English men dressing as women, the Beatles never used drag in their performances. After they stopped touring, their incidental appearances on British TV also abated, so no more skits of *A Midsummer Night's Dream,* which featured a lot of netted chiffon. Even in the movie *Help!,* shot in the Bahamas, their bodies were never the focus. When we did see them shirtless or in bathing suits, what stood out was their lack of muscles, their thin arms and, compared to American examples, their sunken chests. Theirs were English bodies, pale and thin, though John during this time referred to himself as "Fat Elvis."

At first the changes in men's looks were considered radical and subversive. I knew a boy who went to court when his high school banned him from classes because of his long hair; he won the case. Skinny hippie dudes often had their masculinity challenged, the favorite insult being "you faggot," but after Vietnam vets began to grow their hair long and hang beads and buttons on their camo field jackets, the divisions between manliness and unmanliness began to blur. Every American style began to blur: Dylan quickly went from a denim jacket folkie to a leather jacket biker. The West Coast surfer look merged with the cowboy ethos. Professors began to wear turtlenecks with no ties, and if Don Draper's associates are any indication, office attire changed too. Some British bands wore ball-splitting pants that visually asserted their maleness in case their long hair and skinny chests created doubts. Because of mini skirts, women's legs were daily scrutinized. Soon women would go braless. Some male singers began to wear makeup and adopt personas. Afros increased in circumference, and by the end of the 1970s, Robert Mapplethorpe's provocative photograph "Man in Polyester Suit," in addition to being a powerful phallic demonstration of Black Power, brought into question any inherent neutering qualities the business suit was thought to have. Men were letting it all hang out, in more ways than one.

In November 1968, four months before their marriage, possibly in defiance to all this strutting fashion, and perhaps to preempt any prurient expectation the press might have that John and Yoko's honeymoon bed-in event would actually involve fucking, the couple created the original rock and roll selfie: two ordinary bodies stark naked, front and back, on the cover for their album *Unfinished Music No. 1: Two Virgins*. Iconic and notorious, this photograph remains revelatory regarding Lennon's excesses and its lasting power to provoke discomfort in viewers.

If the transposition of lyrics into image accelerates John's confessional mode, the *Two Virgins* photo could be considered predictable instead of excessive. If he can be Nowhere Man, he can also be Naked Man. You say you want a revolution, well, here it is, hairy balls and all. Most disturbing were the comments directed at John and Yoko's bodies, as though worldwide fame is no guard against not being pretty enough. George Harrison remarked that the bodies aren't nice ones, and John himself has called them both ordinary and ugly, by which I think he knew that in the public's eye the ordinary *is* ugly, something much truer today than in 1968.

But unlike today's selfie culture, John and Yoko were not soliciting "likes," nor did they objectify their bodies as pornography. They were, however, selling an album (one that didn't do well), and because the photograph is of two extraordinarily famous people, their bodies carry an aura anonymous bodies can't.

Compared to album covers that came later, *Two Virgins* might be the last time the body of any rock musician was authentically and innocently photographed. The photo has a context but little or no pretext or artifice. To see its negative influence on later album art, all you have to do is go online and check out *Rolling Stone's* list of the twenty dirtiest album covers.

And what did I feel seeing my lovely John letting it all hang out? Beats me; I don't even know when I first saw the photograph, but it was probably some time in the early 1970s, but it could have been later. By then I had become sexually active and seen naked men, so I probably wasn't shocked, but I might have been dismayed. Even with the scant sleeping around I had done, I knew I didn't like hairy balls and John, alas, had hairy balls. And his center-part hairdo makes him look like Prince Valiant instead of a rocker. Stripped of clothing, what category would he fit into? Is this an image of a *Beatle?* The photograph does what it intended: demystify. Too bad I didn't know about demystification back when I started having sex. If I had, I could have saved myself a lot of woe.

But I didn't know. For example, I didn't know that a pimply-faced stocky boy could without warning or hesitation direct my head into his crotch, hold it there with his hand, and stick his dick in my mouth until it spilled over like a chalky-tasting milkshake. D. H. Lawrence hadn't mentioned anything about this. This event happened before I lost my virginity, which I did willingly the following week with the same boy in the same car, only this time I wasn't wearing the sleeveless red print dress my sister had made for me—you know, the dress with golf ball-size buttons down its front, the same buttons that left bruises on my sternum because of how he held me down—I always liked that dress, it was very '60s.

The loss of my virginity was expeditious; I wanted it over with and very quickly it was. We were two virgins, and by silent agreement we knew we'd never see each other again. But the next day, a Saturday, his mother came to the house to return my glasses, which I had left in his car. She gave them to my father, who happened to be out in the yard.

Did I learn anything from these two events? Yes: that you never accelerate before a curve but wait until you're in it, and never trust a man who holds your head down. The driving tip emerged because we had gone to see the movie *A Man and a Woman*—my first foreign-language film. The French are supposed to be experts in oral sex, but my date chose the movie for its car racing. "This makes me hard," he whispered during one speedy scene.

After him, a pattern emerged with my sex partners: get it in, get it in—it was all about the cock, and I did my best to accommodate, but I wasn't having a very good time. I hardly ever saw the *bbb*s because my partners were so avid to have intercourse. Back then the big thrill was doing it in different positions that involved a lot of synchronization; rolling over without disengaging was a sought-after accomplishment, I recall. These adult freedoms were so different from teenage furtiveness, but there was little real pleasure for me except for the fact that I was finally having sex.

Of course my heart got broken; three weeks seemed to be the limit of any involvement, and I always blamed myself for some lack or overeagerness or dependency. Of course I couldn't—no, I didn't even try to—play hard to get, or buy into that demeaning metaphor about milk and cows. I wanted sex, even bad, one-way sex. I carried injectors filled with spermicide in my purse; I read *Tropic of Cancer*. I even asked my mother for advice about my involvement with an older man, my philosophy prof, because I knew that she had had a romance with a Mexican aviator in the 1930s. What did she tell me? That she was a virgin when she married my father, a huge lie that I had figured out years before by counting the months between her marriage and my brother's birth. Premature my ass, Mom.

I was too involved with real male bodies to dream about John Lennon's. He wasn't there, except as background music in the head shops and on car radios. The unexpurgated truth about John hadn't come out yet, the orgies, the violence. America knew him as the man who did the right thing by marrying Cynthia when she became pregnant. But he would leave her and their son Julian after he met Yoko. Unlike some, I understood his choosing Yoko because I was in an unhappy marriage, too. Yoko was a fellow artist, Lennon's soul mate whom he described as "me in drag." They became creative partners, then became lovers, then became parents.

My husband disparaged my talent by "kidding" me that I wrote poems instead of essays. When I told him I was leaving him, he destroyed my typewriter with a hammer. In court, he fought hard for custody of our daughter. Pregnant when I married him, I knew I didn't love him, but because we had been together for months instead of weeks, I felt that something important was happening to me. Initially, I was taken with him. He had a dark, serious undertow, a black Irish allure I found exotic. His experiences moved me. When he was ten, he lost his father to alcoholism. He had served in Vietnam, and when I met him he was ready to go to jail for his political beliefs. But even before we married, I knew I'd made a mistake and that I needed to get out quickly. My exit took three years, and it wasn't pretty.

I avoid thinking about how much I hurt him, but perhaps that's overextending any lasting effect I've actually had on him. He did marry again, happily for the most part. I'm still embarrassed and confused when I think about our marriage, and about me as a young mother. Who was I all those years ago? My husband had hairy balls and a high sperm count and, like John, he did the right thing.

My marriage temporarily erased John, but one of the first things I did after separating from my husband was buy a huge poster of John's face, one of Richard Avedon's black and white portraits. The poster was in a counterculture variety store near the University of Maryland. I bought it during the lost years, those years of what I did lose or almost lost: my mother, my sense of myself, and my daughter. But here was that face, his face. It had come to claim me. Again.

THERE'S A PLACE

I can easily picture my English friend Sarah at age ten alone in her London bedroom worrying about how she'd take care of Mr. Rochester now that he'd gone blind and then a second later contemplating ways she'd murder Cynthia Lennon— poison? lacrosse stick? It's good to have imaginative, precocious friends. I was thirty-five before I read *Jane Eyre*. At ten I was reading *The Adventures of Robin Hood and His Merry Men* and following Prince Valiant in the comics, so I did my part for the empire. But Sarah? Sarah was hardcore. Still ten, while attending Broomfield House elementary school, Sarah became president of the school's Beatles fan club, what she considered an act of public service.

Fan clubs were instrumental to Beatlemania. The first official one was in Liverpool and run by Freda Kelly, who became a loyal and long-term employee of the band. The ones that followed comprised a scattering of schoolrooms, bedrooms, and other teenage hangouts. At Broomfield House, Sarah lined up the letters, posters, and postage stamps, gathered the photographs and other Beatles ephemera. She was in charge. She had a patriotic duty to fulfill. Fifty-two years later, her Delft blue eyes still blazing with indignation, she tells me, *They were ours before you took them from us.*

Sarah has a point. The Beatles conquered her country in 1963, and then in 1964 they conquered mine. Soon they had conquered the entire world. But only England had Swingin' London, and a few years after Broomfield House, my pal Sarah, now a mini-skirted student at St. Paul's School for Girls, partook of a London scene American girls could only dream of.

South of London, some miles from Sarah, my friend Ian watched the Beatles for the first time on television and remembers thinking how authentic they were. To Ian, the Beatles were talented working-class guys who didn't defer to authority or status; they were real, and they were funny. Those two traits resonated. When I told Ian that John's favorite books were the *Just William* series, he let out a little yelp and said, *My God, you're taking me back to my childhood. Stop it.* Books adhere across classes, and so does music.

Bob, another English friend, grew up in Brighton and wasn't permitted to listen to rock and roll in his house, but he remembers his older sister taking him to Elvis movies. Bob became a musician and recording engineer and once saw John Lennon in the hallway of Abbey Road studios. I wish he hadn't told me this over lunch. It's not polite to gape when you're chewing a turkey sandwich.

Bob moved to the States in the '70s. The night of December 8, 1980, around 10:45 p.m. he was driving home while listening to a local DC radio station that played requests. That night the requests were for Lennon songs. In the middle of the playlist, the deejay broke in to say that someone just called the station claiming John had been shot. Was this a sick joke? No; a few minutes later the deejay broke in again and made an official announcement: John was dead.

In America, there's no place more private than the front seat of your car late at night. You're alone, you've got a good station on the radio, it's dark inside and out, and you can have as many Travis Bickle rants as you like, because no one will ever hear them.

I didn't ask Bob what he was thinking as he drove home that night, but I can imagine. Only in America, gun-happy, full-of-weirdos America. Or maybe he thought how strange the layering was of that specific moment on the radio, one so serendipitous he might be tempted to disbelieve in serendipity altogether considering the unlikelihood of hearing Lennon sing and then learning that he'll never sing again. It's enough to make you laugh, something Lennon might have done were he in the car, given how acquainted he was with unexpected death.

Or cry.

Private moments, even for a girl of ten, permit her to claim something of the Beatles for herself that's different from the wider spectacle unleashed by screaming fans. Sarah remembers being secretly happy that her favorite Beatle, John, was "the intelligent one," and in the privacy of her room she drew a parallel between him and the charismatic Mr. Rochester beyond what we might expect of a ten-year-old. Daydreaming encourages such alignments. Bob, like many other young men, made a private aspiration public by forming a band. By virtue of gender, teenage boys could hope to become the Beatles, whereas Sarah and other girls could fantasize only a proximal identification by becoming a Beatle's wife. Regardless of the outcome, privacy of thought and feeling is a guard against all "official" response to experience. After the band broke up, the Beatles industry took off; John's murder predictably intensified this acceleration. More books, more photographs, more exposés, all of which potentially swayed fans to forget one's private experience of the band and identify with whatever published history most suited them. But the opposite was also true. The contested truths about the band, especially who wrote what, along with the intricacies of the recording sessions, elevated Beatles criticism to a new level, and for a certain type of fan, the close textual analysis of Beatles songs, including discussions of psychological differences that could explain artistic differences (e.g., John is "horizontal," Paul is "vertical"), enhanced their private feelings about the band.

"There's a Place" is an early Beatles song that asserts the value of privacy. The "place" is John's mind, where "there's no time / when I'm alone." Sung with great insistence and piercing harmony, for many male critics this song is loaded with significance beyond the usual romantic concerns its lyrics imply, for instance, being blue. For Ian MacDonald, the song represents "a young man's . . . assertion of self-sufficient defiance." Steve Turner hears the lyrics as a search for "comfort," while Tim Riley insists on the song's "innocence." For Geoffrey O'Brien, the song is a "stand in for the overall value of the Beatles . . . [a] sonic environment [that] turned out to be an excellent cure for too much thinking." Robert Christgau hears John's "ability to transcend the isolation he dreads."

Initially, I didn't know what to make of such serious regard for this song. You certainly can't dance to it, and it's quite short. It's one of those quirky Beatles songs that defies category. John dismissed it outright, yet it's impossible to separate John from the song's impact because it's his mind we're going into.

The song's title also invites us into a literal place, John's small, front-facing bedroom in Aunt Mimi's house. That room is the place of his earliest writings, his private thoughts, but also the place he frequently escaped from—to visit his mother, or to try his luck in Hamburg, and later to lay musical claim to the Cavern Club and a sexual claim to its female patrons. In 1960, after the group was kicked out of Hamburg, John, alone, penniless and dejected, returned to this narrow room. It was a young man's room.

♪

The room that is now my study used to be my older brother's bedroom, the smallest of three in our family house. The
original wallpaper was atrocious, tea roses I think, but I
can't remember when it was removed and painted over. I do
remember the photographs of body builders my brother had
pinned to the wall, as he was athletic and intent on gaining
muscle, which he did. He also had his *Outdoor Life* and *Field
and Stream* magazines stacked neatly near his bed. I liked to
snoop in my parents' room, but I never did in my brother's.
Given how masculine it was, how could it hold anything of
interest for me? A neatly tied woolly bugger freshwater fly?
Well, who'd want that?

Now I think very differently about the rooms men occupied as boys. Their earlier ghosts might still be there, along
with some residue of habit, violence, or pattern of thinking.
Bob Dylan entered John's boyhood bedroom just to look out
its window and sit on the edge of the bed. He didn't sit on
that bed because his feet hurt. He was chasing down some
complicated emotion.

After his divorce, my brother would occasionally bring
whatever woman he was dating to the house and show her
his old room. There wasn't anything original to see except
the view out its two windows, but even that had grown less
expansive because the neighbors' trees had grown. Showing
off the bedroom was an intimate act; within its walls, my
brother's past has a place, and here it is. What also matters
about the room is that my brother no longer occupies it. It
measures the distance between the boy who had no choice
regarding where he slept and the man who went on to create
lovely bedrooms in the houses he built for other people.

Intimacy can work collectively as well. A few years ago, I
saw Ashley Gilbertson's book of photographs, *Bedrooms of
the Fallen,* forty images of the bedrooms of soldiers, mostly
young men, who either died in Iraq and Afghanistan or
who committed suicide after returning home. In their still-
ness, these photos convey a reverence created by common-

place, often brand-name items interspersed among personal ones, but the most personal dimension of these rooms, their occupant, is missing. A specific type of young man fills this vacancy: He's a doer, a sportsman, someone who likes action figures and drinks beer, someone who needs to serve a noble cause. He embodies a hypermasculine image of American manhood, one that doesn't always ensure a positive outcome. If a boy adheres to the demands of this image, by leaving his room he will, supposedly, become a man. He also might die. These photographs measure that potential sacrifice by depicting a place of no return.

Some boys don't have a place to call their own. Can we even call the hospital bed Ringo lay in for a year when he was six a room? Would my ex-lover Lucas's prison cell count as a room? He went behind bars when he was seventeen and stayed there for more than ten years. Did my friend Ian's boarding school provide an adequate room for the seven years he was away from his parents' home? Such conditions force a boy to occupy a place within his own mind, to create a world within the world.

It's easy to understand why John Lennon, a boy shuttled here and there by various family members, would become obsessed with a place to call his own. For a few years that place seemed to be a band called the Beatles. Their touring schedule was grueling, creating a forced intimacy that amazingly was mostly trouble free. During the early touring years, they shared hotel bedrooms, making a point to rotate who slept in whose room lest favoritism formed. It was one for all and all for one.

How strange, then, to discover that as a rich man John Lennon generally occupied only two rooms in his twenty-seven-room Weybridge mansion. One room had a ratty sofa where he would sit for hours reading newspapers. The other, his bedroom on an upper level, was furnished very sparsely and had worn rugs on the floor. Unlike today, when celebrities invite TV networks into their homes for a white-glove tour, the Beatles longed for privacy, and John sought it in rumpled rooms.

♪

John Lennon's body was cremated at Ferncliff Cemetery in Westchester County, New York. Many famous entertainers are buried there, among them Thelonious Monk, Jerome Kern, Basil Rathbone, Judy Garland, and Ed Sullivan. We can visit their graves, we know where they are, as even a grave or a crypt is a kind of room. However, in death, John is "roomless," without place. There is no known urn full of his ashes, no niche for that urn in the wall of a columbarium. Wisely, Yoko has kept this information private. If she had given John any kind of final resting place, it would have become overrun with fans, gawkers, and the usual mix of crazies. Olivia Harrison knew this, too. After George was cremated, his ashes were scattered in the Ganges River. No fixed place may be the most private place of all, for both John and his fans. The absence of a fixed location allows for the creation of any number of individual inner places where one could "keep" John. When I listen to a Beatles record on my Walkman, I go to that place—not every time, not if I'm working in the garden or cleaning up, but when I want my singular, inner experience of John, I just stay put and push the earphones tighter against my head and let his voice flood my brain. Private access, private worship. In this aural place, he's all mine.

We understand this. Privacy affords control and protection, exactly what occupants of hospitals, prisons, and boarding schools don't have. Often celebrities don't have it either, which helps explain John's five-year domestic interlude during which he didn't record or perform and became a stay-at-home dad to his son Sean, born in 1975. It explains, too, John's retreat into LSD ten years earlier.

There might also be privacy in Central Park's Strawberry Fields, the two-and-a-half-acre landscaped memorial Yoko and others established in John's memory in 1985. Except for the Imagine Circle, an eleven-foot-wide mosaic of stones, there's no other "official" memorial to Lennon. The site is quiet and peaceful. No photographs of John hang on the walls because there are no walls. Strawberry Fields is a room in nature's house. It's "official," but it's also free. People can think and feel whatever they want. It's the opposite of the huge exhibition, *Lennon: His Life and Work,* Yoko curated for the Rock and Roll Hall of Fame fifteen years later in 2000.

Museums are rooms full of stuff, stuff traditionally dedicated to art. But in keeping with other flashy media, some museums today offer a fuller experience of images, sound, objects, videos, and interactive displays. Too often the contemporary museum experience is geared more toward spectacle than contemplation. In such overwhelming environments, it's difficult to maintain a privacy of mind that allows room for your own thoughts.

I didn't see the Lennon exhibition in Cleveland's Rock and Roll Hall of Fame, only read about it online and in John Kimsey's essay "Spinning the Historical Record, Lennon, McCartney, and Museum Politics." Mounted to commemorate what would have been John's sixtieth birthday, and filling three floors, this exhibition was a public assemblage of mythic proportions. The myth I have in mind is the death and re-membering of Osiris by his wife, Isis.

Kimsey describes the entry into the exhibit as "a walk-in triptych with a large bed . . . on the right, a . . . panel featuring the numeral '60' in the center, and on the left an orange column . . . towering roughly ten to twelve feet high." We are entering a tomb, one that charges admission.

In Egyptian mythology, Osiris is murdered and his body parts are strewn across the land. Isis, his wife, collects the parts and through her powers restores her husband's body. It's a skewed Humpty-Dumpty tale, one with fancy gold headdresses and big jewelry. Mounted with Yoko's flair for drama and exposure, the exhibition becomes rather icky. In addition to the expected objects on display, such as lyric sheets, photographs, and guitars, there are troubling personal items: the bloodstained eyeglasses John was wearing the night he was killed and a brown paper bag the police gave to Yoko containing the clothes he wore that night. Given her long-standing interest in Egyptian art and culture, Yoko has, in good Isis fashion, accumulated and reconstituted her dead husband—for a public, paying audience. For the price of admission, anyone can see John's blood.

Yoko is the prime guardian of the Lennon myth. But by displaying John's bloody glasses (if indeed they are the real thing and not a replica), she panders to those fans who see Lennon not as a man but as a religious deity whose relics and fetishes are stand-ins for his absent body. Perhaps this was her intention, to keep the myth and selected artifacts always in circulation. The same kind of revitalizing happened in 1995 for the Beatles *Anthology,* when two Lennon songs, "Free as a Bird" and "Real Love," were released posthumously via the "magic" of digital remastering, in effect bringing John's voice back from the dead to join once again with the Beatles.

There's a difference between someone's blood and someone's voice. John's fans have always known him through his voice, one that technology made public through records, films, and interviews. The vocal aspect of his body, along with thousands of images, created a visible and bodily-present public Lennon millions felt they knew and loved, I among them. Blood, however, is interior, usually invisible, and exclusive to the body it inhabits. Blood is private; it may be the most private part of us. Its proper place is within our bodies. By violating this privacy, Yoko commodifies John's blood at the same time she makes it sacred. Something tells me that John wouldn't have approved of Yoko doing this.

Perhaps I'm being too hard on Yoko here. With John no longer present, all she has are his things, and like the parents of the soldiers in Ashley Gilbertson's book she has created a place for them that she has decided to share with others. Widows are known to keep the pillowcase their husbands used to sleep on as an olfactory reminder of the husband's absent body. But the widow does this in private. It's the public and sensational nature (not to mention the capitalistic motive) of what Yoko does that puts me off. John already looms so visibly and psychically huge on the cultural landscape that each of us can *re-member* him according to our own desires. Likewise, Yoko can claim her private John, as is her right, perhaps her obligation, to do so.

When does the grieving widow wash her husband's pillowcase, if she ever does? I knew a woman whose father, a policeman, was killed on duty. For years, she kept a shovel in the trunk of her car because she often had the urge to go to his grave and dig up his body, she missed him that much. In time, the shovel became as important as her father because it was a physical link to a once physical being. Working their here/not here effect on us, photographs are also physical links, ones we welcome and control, even slip between plastic to keep dust-free or hang on our wall. The photograph I took of John when I saw the Beatles live in the Ed Sullivan studio on August 14, 1965, is kept in a place only I know about. My private ghost.

In another drawer, lying on a piece of gray foam cushion inside a tiny dentist's box, is a large yellow molar. Charles's tooth. It's a body part of a man I loved for over nine years until his death. Charles was thirty-five years my senior and in poor health, but when love calls, you answer the phone. We were in love and very good for each other. I mention this not to draw a parallel to John and Yoko's unusual attachment but in support of their union, which many people disapproved of. Charles's tooth, like John's bloody glasses, tells a story, and here it is in a poem I wrote:

LITTLE BONE

Little bone, only bone that's left, wee, hard thing,
pissed-colored, forked, gold topped and odorless,
how can I make a man of you, a body and a voice,
when I forgot for all these years where I had put you—
in the nonsense drawer along with half-wrapped
lozenges, extra buttons and a green shoelace.

Worse than any burial.

But worse still that you should be reborn
in such crude ceremony, my nesting
instinct in reverse telling me to dump the junk.

That's how you tumbled back,
a solid clatter on the floor.
Now what, I thought, and kneeling to the noise
found you instead.

Oh bone, scruple weighing down my tongue, it all comes
                                                    back:
Charles, cotton-jawed and woozy in the dentist's chair,
and you, abandoned near the blood-pinged instruments.

I took you then,
slipped you in my pocket like a piece of stolen candy,
thinking, *how romantic, how unladylike*
to hold this part of him not even I had tasted.

And then: I forgot you.

Little bone, for the dust and darkness you have lasted
through, forgive me. It was a difficult time and, always,
so much to remember.

I can only imagine what Yoko Ono has to remember. But unlike me, I doubt she's forgotten any part of it.

AEOLIAN CADENCES

Never marry a musician. That could be the subtext of my mother's marriage, and it's surely the main text of Cynthia Lennon's. But what's the text for the long-term nonmatrimonial live-in partnership I have with my music man? I've kept my own money and independence, and there are no children to contend with, so perhaps the text is *love*? But it could just as easily be insanity, the hair-tearing, breast-beating (and breast-baring) insanity women have felt for musicians since the time of Beethoven and Liszt, probably since some Arcadian ephebe struck a chord on his homemade lyre.

Insanity, not love, explains the night I wanted to stab The Man I Love (TMIL) with the long-handled, two-prong BBQ fork we keep in the drawer near the stove, a place I now see as an arsenal of domestic weaponry. What drove me to that drawer, you ask? We were arguing about Aeolian cadences. Yes, that.

I'm pretty sure neither my mother nor Cynthia Lennon ever used kitchen weaponry against their husbands, and I'm certain they never argued about Aeolian cadences. That honor is all mine. My father played the trombone professionally, and unless he was practicing scales in the basement, the instrument stood mute in its huge case, sealed in pharaonic mystery next to the water meter. There was nothing musically for my mother and father to argue about since she played piano and was somewhat knowledgeable about music. But I'm not that knowledgeable, so I depend on TMIL to answer any question I may have. Most times this Q & A is quick and satisfying, but when it's not . . .

I was reading Ian MacDonald's *Revolution in the Head,* that sacred text about all Beatles songs. In his discussion of "Not a Second Time," a 1963 Lennon tune, MacDonald mentions an article by William Mann, then classical music critic for the London *Times.* In Mann's article, he asserts that the song ends with an Aeolian cadence, the same as in Mahler's "Song of the Earth," and goes on to say that John and Paul must "think simultaneously of harmony and melody."

Mann, like many after him, strained to make Beatles music "legitimate," something any Brit under twenty-two at the time would have considered superfluous. Unlike Mann, younger listeners probably knew that John and Paul sang close harmony *a la* the Everly Brothers, along with a splash of English/Irish folk song modality and Anglican hymns. In his 1980 *Playboy* interview, John settled the matter by saying he had no idea what Aeolian cadences are and that to him "they sound like exotic birds." A signature Lennon quip, one that strikes a deathblow to intellectual blather. Trouble is, sometimes I like intellectual blather, and so does MacDonald, whose book is full of musical terms that to the common reader probably seem as mysterious as my father's trombone.

So, one night I innocently asked The Man I Love: *Darling, what are Aeolian cadences?*

—*There's no such thing as an Aeolian cadence.*

—*But it says right here*—

—*the book's wrong, Aeolian cadences don't exist*—

—*But the critic*—

—What's the context, who's the composer?
—Well, it's this Beatles song—
—Oh, god, no wonder—
—The classical critic—
—doesn't know shit—
—of the London Times, I could play you the record—
This is a safe place to stop, but we'll return in a bit.

Military men, salesmen, musicians—these are long-standing categories of male separateness, husbands and fathers who leave the home for periods of time and then return. These absences congeal into a reputation or a cliché: a sailor with a sweetheart in every port; the same for the drummer in a touring rock band. The salesman who has an entire family in another city. My mother didn't suffer this kind of subterfuge because by the time she and Daddy married in 1944, his years of touring with big bands had ended. After he joined the US Army Band, he stayed home composing and doing arrangements. From time to time, he'd haul his trombone up from the basement for a paying gig, and sometimes my mother would go with him. But she didn't like being a "band widow" clumped around a table with the other widows hawk-eyeing the bar for groupies hitting on their husbands.

From the beginning, loneliness defined Cynthia Lennon's marriage to John, and as the Beatles became more famous, her loneliness increased. In her memoir *John*, Cynthia reveals how he returned exhausted from touring and would sleep for days. The lyrics to "I'm Only Sleeping" from *Revolver* may seem innocent to some but certainly not to Cynthia and their son, Julian, who had to live with a zonked and emotionally absent John after he began using LSD. It never got better. When Cynthia remarked that John wrote songs for her, she was gauging their marriage in musical terms, a poignantly ironic measurement that would later require another question: if Cynthia wasn't his inspiration, then who was or would be?

—Could I at least read you the passage?

By now I'm waving both MacDonald's book and a copy
of Mann's article that I had downloaded.

—*No*

—*OK, here's the passage from MacDonald*—

—*Oh, god, OK read it*

So I read it, and TMIL says

—*MacDonald's wrong*

—*It's not MacDonald; he's quoting the critic*

—*These guys don't know shit. Aeolian is not a cadence*

—*it's a quote, here's the entire article*

—*don't bother, Law and Order's on*

—*How do you know the critic's wrong? Maybe you're
wrong.*

If John's MO was sleep, my parents' was silence. I never
heard them argue, just grumbled asides from my mother. My
father had the ability to float above everything, taking walks
at night and listening to records through headphones. He put
up barriers to any dispute, and my mother was probably too
tired to raise issues. Me and TMIL? We yell, snarl, hiss, and
every time he says "stop, enough" I keep at it. I'm not proud
of this, but our arguments over music, however full of invec-
tive, are a form of intimacy, one as exclusive as sex because I
only fight this way with you-know-who.

Like my father, and probably like John, TMIL lives in his
head because that's where the music is, and arguing gets him
out of his head. Unlike my father, TMIL is not a composer;
he's a player and a consummate listener. A CAT scan of his
brain would contain a note-for-note catalogue of Western
music, not all of course, but a great deal. Just the other night,
we made the mistake of watching *Woman in Gold*, a drippy
film about repatriating Gustav Klimt's famous painting back
to the surviving member of the original family who owned
it. A brief scene takes place in a Vienna concert hall. Two
notes in and TMIL says, "Oh, that's Schoenberg's 'Transfig-
ured Night.'" The same thing happens while listening to the

jazz station in the car. Who's that playing the sax, I'll ask, and immediately he tells me.

This ability drives me nuts. First of all, it's totally sexy to be right so often, to have such knowledge, to know how someone uses his mouth to make music. Second, it indicates a lifetime of dedication toward one's art. Third, he's sharing this knowledge with *me*. I fantasize a lot about having deep D. H. Lawrence-type talks about art and life with The Man I Love, conversations I know seldom occur with anyone in real life, let alone a domestic partner. Trouble is (there's that phrase again), I want TMIL to fantasize about having these conversations, too, to be turned on by what I know about the music I like. Damn it, I want him to like my music, because dismissing it dismisses me. There it is in all its ugliness, my fascistic fantasy of what makes a good conversation.

—*Maybe you're wrong* I repeated *it's possible, you know*

—*Lennon knows nothing and I'm not wrong*

—*you're not listening to me, Lennon's dissing the critic you jerk*

—*and what have I always told you about critics, what did Stravinsky say about critics*

—*I know, I know, but can't you see that Lennon's on your side, all the terminology—*

—*like exotic birds? That certainly furthers musical theory. Jeez, what a fool—*

—*you're doing this on purpose, like you always do*

By this time, we're both on our feet, eyeing each other like Sumo wrestlers going for the lunge. The Man I Love is dissing another man I love, and I can't let that happen.

So I say

—*he's not a fool, you're missing his humor, he's admitting he doesn't know*

—*well, he's right about that.*

—*What's the term mean! That's all I wanted to know.*

—*There is no term Aeolian cadence because there is no Aeolian cadence.*

—*Well, it says right here, why don't you read it for yourself*—

and I wave MacDonald's book at him again

—*Oh great,* Revolution in the Head, *that's helpful.*

—*He's also written about Shostakovich*

—*Do I give a crap?*

—*You always do this. It's always your music and not mine. Why can't you take the Beatles seriously?*

—*I don't like the Beatles.*

—*You like "Blackbird."*

—*That's McCartney, he's written some good melodies*—

—*just because Herbie Hancock played it. If it's jazz then it's all good, but if it's rock, it's crap. You're just an old fogey.*

—*I'm talking about musical integrity*—

—*Paul's got the melodies, sure, but John's got the feelings*—

—*Who cares about feelings? Music is absolute. It is what it is.*

Let's stop for a moment to consider this phrase: *Music is absolute.* What does that mean? Can it mean anything? And what about *It is what it is?* To even consider such a statement is to invite the void, a swirling endless tape loop worse than anything John and Yoko produced while on acid. Yet TMIL inserts this dead-end koan into our conversations with regularity, which, of course, drives me nuts.

However, music being absolute does mean something, I think, in the way that a code must be absolute, or an intricate machine, or a Bach sonata. There's no such thing as a wrong note, but the trick to creating great music is to know which *right* note comes next. The Man I Want to Stab with a Fork taught me this. So, it must have been out of concern for precision that he calmly (the calm of a hit man going about his business) said to me

—*There's no such thing as Aeolian cadences because the word Aeolian describes one of the seven modes of music, and modes are not cadences.*

Well, that settles it, doesn't it? And off he goes down into the basement (the very same basement that housed my father's trombone), to his man cave of CDs, musical scores, instruments, tiny bristled brushes used to clean the holes in his flute or clarinet—or maybe just to remove ear wax, I don't know, because he's very protective of his basement possessions such as the slivered reeds in the Sucrets tin, the one white cotton velvet glove, even the miscellaneous pencil shavings and loose, mysterious metal bolts—they all call for a certain propriety or reverence, like a Joseph Cornell world spread out across the length of a glass-topped bookcase beneath our basement window. From this bookcase he brings me Elvo S. D'Amante's *All About Chords,* which lists the seven modes, Aeolian among them. I was no closer to understanding what Aeolian means, but I was satisfied that our argument had ended.

At what point in the argument did the BBQ fork I wanted to stab TMIL with enter my mind? I don't remember, but the thought of it fathered no deed. Am I even capable of jabbing two prongs into human flesh while screaming *A fork is a fork is a fork you motherfucker?* I doubt it. Careful not to overestimate my capabilities, I try to keep the part of my mind that contains such imaginings at a distance, like a curious insect specimen I'll look at but won't touch. Empirical knowledge is useful, but sometimes the wish suffices.

Every marriage is a mystery, to both participants and observers. By early 1963, John and Cynthia's marriage was impacted by the public frenzy of Beatlemania. Brian Epstein kept Cynthia secreted from the fans and the press lest they discovered John was a husband and a father. She was not released from her purdah until the band's 1964 American tour, the first and last time she went on tour with the Beatles. For years, John treated Cynthia terribly, but his ill treatment sprang the escape hatch on his marriage. Before John met Yoko Ono, he was deeply unhappy, barricaded within Kenwood, his twenty-seven-room mansion in Weybridge filled with all kinds of stuff: a gorilla costume, a suit of armor, juke-boxes, slot machines, a church altar, none of which made him happy except, perhaps, his miniature race car sets. John was the Nowhere Man of his song, which he wrote while living at Kenwood. By the time Yoko fully inserted herself between John and Cynthia, behavior he encouraged, John had entered another mode, an entire tonal shift of artistic direction and self-exploration. Cynthia didn't change modes; she lived for their son Julian and set about giving him as normal a life as possible, one containing a final, painful irony: she was instrumental to one of John's best songs, "The Ballad of John and Yoko," a narrative of his and Yoko's wedding day on March 20, 1969, a song made possible by Cynthia granting him a divorce. She lives in the negative space of that hit single, of his new beginning from the ruins of her faithful love.

I don't know what Cynthia did with the items John left in Kenwood. I imagine when he left that he took only what mattered most to him: his instruments, books, records, his two paintings by Stuart Sutcliffe, the usual items a male musician might value. After John departed, the house must have sounded different, no low-droning TV for one thing, no whistling or any of the voices he was capable of mimicking. The variations of his breathing, the sound his weight made on the stairs, all the aural evidences of their life together, happy and unhappy, would be gone. Perhaps she was relieved.

My mother couldn't have escaped her marriage even if she wanted to. However, soon after her death, my father began preparing a new life for himself, one that involved two new wives in succession, which meant that he had two willing sets of ears to tell his story to, the good times he had had on the road, the famous people he had played with, the music he loved and heard. I've heard these stories, too; I've repeated them to TMIL. These stories allowed me to imagine a possible way of life centered on doing creative work and getting paid for it. And if that wasn't possible, then living with and respecting the creative efforts of others: as my father taught me, always put the record back in its album cover; respect the artifact, respect the artist.

I remember too the shock I and my siblings felt when we discovered, after our father's death, that he had been married before he married our mother. His first wife had been a singer with the band, a sexy blonde wearing a sequined snood straight out of prewar couture. Daddy had kept the photograph with him all through his marriage to our mother. Then we learned that during the war he had fathered an illegitimate daughter. Then we learned that our mother knew all of this and had made Daddy promise never to tell us kids. Those were the days when "divorce" was a whispered word and "bastard child" an unthinkable phrase. At the heart of my parents' marriage was a promise premised on shame, and learning of this sent me reeling. But it didn't keep me off musicians.

Some years back, love was not good to me. I felt a loneliness I could not abide or explain. When The Man I Love was out of the house, often on a gig, I'd go into the basement and stand in front of his CDs, his books, then I'd go upstairs and open his closet door and just look at the clothes that hung there. I wanted him gone. I wanted him to stay forever. My heart was turning to sand, that's how angry and confused I was, but I could do nothing. He was of little help. Maybe he was turning to sand, too. I never asked.

Every day during that time, he played his flute down in the basement, something he still does today. The notes, winding through the air ducts and registers, reached me in my upstairs study, a sound that would become as essential to me as the heat it rode upon. One day I tiptoed halfway down the basement steps, just enough so that when I sat on the step and bent my head past the beam I could see him from the waist down. There he was, his legs, at least. I didn't need to see more of him because I already knew how he held his instrument, how he stood before the tall black music stand, how straight his back was, the delicacy of his wrists and his long fingers, his embouchure, that kiss on silver. I wanted him gone, but if he left so would the music. Then the entire world would turn to sand.

Love inhabits the distance between a wish and a fact, a space held in place by the competing gravities of joy and disappointment. He stayed. I stayed. Somehow we've managed. We've turned the record over. We've put a new one on. Somewhere in this lovely mess, the exotic birds are tuning up for their next number.

TRUTH OR BEAUTY

John Lennon wrote "How Do You Sleep?" with a knife. Featured on his 1971 *Imagine* album, the song slams Paul McCartney who, on December 31, 1970, had gone to court to dissolve their legal partnership. One listen is all you need to get the song's meaning: Lennon's pissed, and to hell with a fifteen-year friendship. Yet, despite John's anger and hurt, the knife doesn't cut all the way through. Yes, he's cut Paul, but he hasn't fatally cut him off, or cut him out of his life. He's still singing to him, and as long as he keeps singing, friendship is still possible.

I wish I could say the same about my ex-friend Brenda. Eleven years ago, she ended our friendship with an email, and when I reached out to her she refused communication. I had been cast aside like a piece of junk mail, but that's an after-the-fact simile. When it actually happened, I felt like I'd been shoved out of an airplane. Compared to the Beatles' tsunami-size breakup, my ordeal with Brenda is a grain of sand disturbed by an ocean breeze. Nevertheless, there are similarities.

Over fifty years ago, I chose John over Paul and became a John girl. My high school friend Betty was a Paul girl. At the time, my choice felt instinctive, but now I believe it was more than that. Whom we desire at fifteen, and why, can be the first of many choices that contribute to one's moral code, which over time solidifies into a conduct of life. When I chose John over Paul, I was choosing truth over beauty. It was a choice that made me take sides: John's humor and acerbity against Paul's sentimentality and charm; John's toughness over Paul's niceness. By choosing John, I might not have known that I was merging style with substance, but I did know that truth and beauty were sometimes fungible: John wrote and sang tender songs, and Paul could rip it up with the best of them. Life, like Beatles albums, had room for truth *and* beauty. Nevertheless, my preference for John's truth was a defining moment, one that began my own process of self-definition.

The slow burn of the Beatles' demise is well documented. Feelings of disrespect, the limits of collaboration, and artistic differences began to infect the group. There had always been a healthy competition between John and Paul, fueled as much by yearly contractual demands to create new songs as by their egos, but by the summer of 1966, after recording *Revolver,* tensions escalated. The band kept together, but only for three more years. When the break did occur, it was over money, just as with many marriages. When the end came, millions mourned. The '60s had ended. Truth-teller John would soon sing about the dream being over, and indeed it was.

Female friendships are different from men's. Men are more straightforward, they say what's on their minds, and if no one turns homicidal, life goes back to normal. Even after they broke up, the Beatles continued to play with one another. Paul frequently voiced his wish that the group would get back together and tour, an optimistic, perhaps self-serving wish that both George and Ringo made clear would never come true. John was off with Yoko, handling the pain of the breakup in his usual way, with anger and drugs.

Compared to men, women are more occluded. Their displeasures with each other may never get aired. Often there's only an atmospheric change, a cloudy silence that settles over everything, or the uncomfortable distance measured in small steps when one circles a grievance instead of advancing straight toward it. At least Brenda made her grievance known. I had given her a first draft of a story I had written, which she found insulting. She sent me an email telling me so, but when I called her to talk it over, she never called back. I called three times, but because of her intransigence we never discussed my story or her reaction to it. If we had, I might have pointed out that as a writer herself she was guilty of what she accused me of, namely, writing about real people in a less than flattering way, though I never wrote unflatteringly about her in my story. Perhaps she didn't want to hear this from me. Or perhaps the story was the tangible trespass she needed to justify severing our friendship, something I suspected she'd wanted to do for some time. Either way, her refusal to communicate with me meant that neither of us would sort out our anger and hurt face-to-face. She might have been nonplussed by the situation, but I was in a freefall.

I've often wondered if it would have been better if I had done what John did in 1969. Furious that Paul had missed a recording session, he rushed to Paul's house and during their argument destroyed a painting of his that he had given Paul as a gift. When you think about it, John's was a very feminine response—when angry, destroy something of yourself. But it was also very masculine in its violence. Unlike John, I didn't have the nerve to go to Brenda's house, though many times I imagined me doing so, right down to the dialogue that would ensue. Had I gone, I'm pretty certain she wouldn't have let me in. And there I'd be, an ineffectual loser standing on the sidewalk, my presence a reminder of her resolve and my failed wishful thinking.

Abandoned by Brenda, I was left to wrestle with an absence that quickly filled with more questions than answers.

Were we ever really close friends? I think so. We must have been; we'd had twenty years of friendship, hadn't we? I was twelve years older than her, but age didn't seem to matter. We met in college, were united in our love for poetry and committed to being writers. She was not a Beatles fan, but our musical tastes didn't matter, only the passion with which we held them. We supported each other's creative projects and often shared the stage at readings. There was competition between us, given that one year I'd win a prize and she'd win the next year, but we urged each other on. After all, we were friends, weren't we?

During one of our pot-and alcohol-fueled afternoons, Brenda and I discussed truth and beauty. I asked her what she wanted more: to be respected or to be adored? She didn't hesitate: adored. It was the answer I expected, not only because she had absorbed the Catholic fundamentals of adoration, but because she secularized them so well by dressing the iconic opposite of the holy Virgin. In tight leather skirts, heeled boots, fishnet stockings, big hair, and jangling bangles, she looked the perfect anti-Madonna, all the way down to her pronounced aversion to ever having children. She was great. Everybody loved her. I loved her. She was sexy, funny, hard-working, generous, and multi-talented. Being her friend gave me a certain status and made me feel special.

Everyone wants to be desired—I hope I get invited to the party!—but to be adored is a more exacting thing. There are certain requirements one must properly fulfill when one adores. Adoration requires a specific focus, one that often obliterates. Does the subject of that focus expand or narrow? Does that focus allow for any change or challenge? Brenda is not unusual in wanting to be adored; millions of women want that. A man declaring he'd crawl through glass for her didn't seem to disturb her. Ouch, I thought, who'd want to be the cause of someone doing that? Where is the truth in such a display? But I understood that ethos. It springs from chivalry, gets a refueling at Wuthering Heights, then a literal glass-shattering demonstration in *Body Heat* and any number of contemporary movies that feature hot female stars. If adoration is scripted and takes practice, then feeling adored depends on the mirror. When this affirmation happens, it becomes a self-reflection the adored never tires of and may become dependent on. Who am I if I'm not adored?

Many young females adored the Beatles and performed the required rituals: screaming, throwing Jelly Babies, keeping vigil, and, on one occasion, climbing through Paul McCartney's bathroom window to steal a sacred relic—a beloved photograph of his father. But the Beatles didn't want to be adored, they wanted to be heard. The screaming girls and bruising candy were the reason they stopped performing live. The limitations of adoration led them straight to the studio, where they created incredible music despite the escalating differences between them. You only get respected if you get heard.

In answer to my question, I told Brenda I wanted to be respected. Respect is more truthful, but it doesn't carry the special kick of adoration. How many paintings are there of respect? Respect requires less dramatic validations and doesn't lend itself to snazzy actions. What's the respectful equivalent to crawling through glass? Is there one? I defined respect thusly: to be loved for *me,* to be known and still be loved, to be taken seriously, to not be required to fit a particular mode or model of femininity. To be *true.*

That afternoon's conversation with Brenda became our Keatsian moment, and we agreed that I was Truth and she was Beauty—*that's all ye know of earth, and all ye need to know.* It was a good combination. It worked for us. After all, we both wrote poetry, and we were friends.

I also remember another conversation we once had. She told me how, as a teenager, she decided that she needed to be the hottest girl in the room. When I met her, Brenda was in her twenties, and even in her forties, she continually turned heads. I appreciated her honesty because women aren't always so open about their competitiveness or the effort they put into their presentation. I'm not even sure if it was competitiveness in her case; perhaps it was just an acknowledgement of one common way women get ahead—by being hot. Yet her admission always rankled me, because her need to be the hottest girl in the room also meant, on some level, that I wasn't, and though being hot was not a specific goal of mine, I was never completely comfortable being in her hot shadow.

Over the years something changed in our going-out dynamic. It could have been our age difference finally bearing down with all its social pressure and significance: twelve years' difference *shows,* even in dimly lit bars. I began to feel sidelined. I had moments of jealousy. I grew hyperconscious of our interaction. When we were in public, Brenda never tempered her presentational superiority, and though I knew there was no justification that she do that, it rankled me. We'd be sitting together at a bar, and on more than one occasion the bartender would give Brenda a free drink but not me. I expected her to protest and insist I get one too, but she never did. After a while, whenever we went out, that free drink always seemed to be there, in one form or another.

Women are always in some kind of hierarchy, whether it be one of body type, age, money, number of lovers, level of education, number of publications, number of hours in labor, or who has the biggest orgasm. Friendships can exist within these various hierarchies because women tend to acknowledge their unfulfilled dreams and secret envies to each other. If done sincerely, these admissions can deepen friendship. Brenda used to tell me she envied my nose and skin, and she once caressed my fat butt because she wanted to feel how firm it was. This did surprise me because she has a fabulous backside, one I wouldn't dare touch, though I've often wanted to. We operated along a seeing/touching axis: she demanded immediate visual acknowledgement via her dress and the shapeliness of her body, and I loved looking at her. She was also interested in touching my body. When I modeled for a full-body cast our women artist friends were making, and before they began to lay the plaster strips on me, Brenda asked if she could feel my breast, and I said yes. We both have big breasts, but mine are bigger and older, and as she felt mine she remarked how soft they were compared to hers. There wasn't anything sexual in her touch, but it was fundamentally different from the feel of the other women's hands putting cold, wet plaster on my naked, Vaselined body. Brenda wanted information for herself, and I was happy to give it to her. But I knew if I had asked to feel her breasts, she would have said no. Her ideal was to be seen, not touched, or at least not be touched by women.

Intimate moments such as these probably never happened between the Beatles, I'm sure, though they were in close bodily contact for years. Their sleeping arrangements in Hamburg provided no privacy for fucking, and there was lots of fucking, sharing of girls and sharing of beds. They used sinks in public lavatories for bathing. Before they became famous, they toured in a van and with each bump and turn rolled all over each other like puppies. When in Liverpool, they lived at home, but there were alleys, cars, and dressing rooms for sex. Did they discuss their bodies with each other, compare them the way women do? I doubt it. Did they touch each other out of curiosity? Probably not. Did one of them dress differently to attract attention? Was one hotter than the other three? I doubt it. The only example of bodily envy I'm aware of is the speculation that Pete Best, the drummer before Ringo, was let go because John and Paul were supposedly envious of the attention he got from the female fans. Pete was good-looking in that Tony Curtis kind of way of the late '50s, and he refused to get a Beatles haircut, but it's ludicrous to think the future configuration of the band was premised on envy.

Sexual envies also didn't seem to trouble the Beatles. Though Paul was rumored to be a prolific womanizer, the other three were not in competition with him. No one seemed to be notching his cock; being a Beatle was a notched cock all by itself. Their jealousies and anger resulted over art: Paul asking Yoko, after John's death, if she'd change the song-writing credit for "Yesterday" from Lennon/McCartney to McCartney/Lennon. Ringo storming out during a recording session for the *White Album,* and George, during the filming of *Let It Be,* speaking sarcastically to Paul when he got too bossy. All four Beatles had solo albums at the ready to fill the recording gap after they disbanded. It wasn't looks or sex that antagonized them but artistic endeavor, the last chord spliced and heard four ways.

Before Brenda broke with me, I had concerns about our friendship, small hurts I had not forgotten. Why no thank-you card from her for my wedding present? Why so many unreturned phone calls and emails, the last-minute cancel-lations of invitations? Why the huge snub she gave me at a literary event where we served on the same panel? Why the absence of face time? Yet even as I felt her distance, I was cre-ating some of my own. Was I adequately thrilled about her upcoming marriage? Probably not, though I listened care-fully to her decorating plans. When she waggled her diamond engagement ring at me, I didn't ooh and ah. I don't approve of diamonds; men die digging for them. In this respect, I sup-pose I was a bad female friend, but all my friends know my feelings about marriage and weddings; besides, it was her third marriage. I *was* happy that she was marrying a man who loved her, and the fact that he was well-off didn't really provoke the jealousy it could have. I had also gained some money from one relationship I had been involved in, so I knew the value of money.

The story I wrote and sent to Brenda was the proverbial last straw. I had already read a rough draft aloud to her, and then I sent her a better draft, not the finished story. Though the story was not about Brenda, its setting was a garden party she had hosted, and there were allusions to people who were there. The main thrust of the story was how the main character felt disconnected from people and, ultimately, from the world itself. In hindsight, I should never have shown Brenda the draft, and at the time I was blind to the possibility that in using her party as a setting I was committing a trespass that would hurt or anger her. I wanted to share the story, to have her respond to its force, and I have no regrets about *writing* it, though I gravely miscalculated the effect it would have on her. I wrote my story during the same time that Brenda was writing a novel, one whose characters were based on people we both knew. We knew that writers, especially in first novels, write about what and who they know. But my story must have touched a nerve in Brenda somewhat deeper than the one that makes authors look over their shoulders whenever they write about real people, though she never told me what nerve I had hit. According to the email she sent me, I had commandeered the occasion of her party for my own purposes, and by doing so insulted her family. Guilty on the commandeering; I attempted to turn life into art. Not guilty on the insult. Regardless, I had lost a friend.

After I read her email I was in a panic. My first impulse was to fire off a lengthy rebuttal to her message, but another friend urged me not to do anything in the heat of the moment. In other words, do not behave like John when he rushed to Paul's house and destroyed one of his own paintings. Instead, be cool; be smart. Be powerful, which is the same as cautioning me not to act on the truth of whatever emotions I was then feeling.

I made three phone calls, all picked up by her answering machine, all of which went unreturned. Through friends, I learned that she was hurt that I hadn't apologized for writing the story. But I had promised myself: only three calls, only three messages. I've never stuck to anything like that before in my life. In the past, when a love affair went wrong, there was no end to my self-debasement, my pleading, my making my point. Fortunately, in the years I knew Brenda, I had learned some things from her, one of which was to recognize my own power—she once told me, *Sibbie, you don't know how powerful you are*—so, as any cool lover would have done, I finally held back. As much as I was willing to reach out, to go dramatic if need be, throw stones at her window, maybe even crawl through glass in order to have my say in the matter, and to listen to hers, I didn't budge: three calls and no more. I waited, but I got nothing.

Her refusal to meet with me canceled any merging of truth and beauty—the truth of what really happened and our feelings about it, and the beauty of forgiveness, understanding, and possible reconciliation. Her continued silence forestalled any future reconciliation. Over time I began to feel, and still do, that I came through this ordeal the better person. What kind of person zaps a twenty-plus-year friendship without any explanation or face-to-face meeting? When I considered this question, I realized that I had capacities Brenda didn't have; for one, the capacity to talk over a difficult issue. I also realized that she might be afraid of me, that the power she always urged me to embrace was actually there and that she didn't want to have to face it.

The trouble between me and Brenda had a ripple effect that complicated friendships with four other friends, all writers, who had also collaborated on artistic projects and happily socialized for years. That wonderful web of friendship changed after Brenda's email. Since she refused to be in the same room with me, I wasn't invited to one friend's birthday party, which hurt me and put my friend on the spot. Whatever previous friendly configurations were in place within the group before Brenda dismissed me shifted for a while, and everyone became awkward and tiptoey. Everyone got tired of my fixation on the problem, including me, and after two years (yes, it took that long), the group's dynamics evened out and I quit thinking so much about Brenda. The group, sans Brenda, is stronger than ever. I'm stronger, too. I kept true to my truth: friends don't refuse to meet and discuss difficult matters. They should face head-on whatever difficulties are between them. When Brenda didn't call me back, I held firm. Call it my Paul moment—I will give no more, so let the breakup ensue.

After these years without Brenda, I still wonder if she misses my truth, the different rhythms of my intellect and manner of speaking, my humor, and what in the past she's called my courage and fortitude. I know I miss her beauty. I've no one to discuss poetry with, or to gleefully dissect sexual escapades we've had in the past. Or to smoke dope and giggle with. On paper, poetry, sex, and pot don't seem like much of a foundation for a friendship, but of course there was much more than that, all the inescapable yet evaporative nuances of every encounter we had had, the countless little things you like about a person without even noticing that you like them. These are what you miss. These are what kept Paul visiting John in New York in the 1970s and what hurt him when John, after Sean was born, asked Paul to call before coming over. The rhythms of their friendship had changed, but it's nice to think that had John not been murdered, Paul and he would have found a new rhythm that kept their friendship alive, even if an offbeat one.

But maybe Brenda didn't see me as I saw her. Maybe, when the time came, I was easily replaced, perhaps even erased from her past as she moved into her future.

Some years back, I had to be photographed for a magazine that was publishing an essay I'd written. Brenda wanted to do my makeup for the photo shoot, so she came to my house. Between my cosmetics and what she'd brought, she had plenty to work with. I sat in a chair near a sunlit window, and she leaned close to my face applying foundation, shadow, and gobs of mascara. And then bright lipstick carefully applied, blotted, then reapplied and sealed. She wanted to make me beautiful, to look good for the camera, a very loving project she took on. She did improve me. I was officially made up. Then she packed her box and off she went. *Smile, sweetie,* she said, and waved.

When she left, I looked again at myself in the mirror. Yes, I was vibrant, perhaps even sophisticated, but something was off, I just didn't feel like myself, my true self. It was the lipstick; she'd put on too much, and the liner extended beyond my natural lips. Brenda had given me her lips, those bad-girl lips. I took a tissue and wiped off as much of the color as I could, not because I didn't appreciate Brenda fixing me up, but because I wanted the face in the photograph to look like mine. To look like me. Me.

BLOKES

My standard Beatles fantasy is this: a limousine pulls up in front of my house and either John or Paul steps out and sweeps up my front walk. Whoever's at my door I ask in, we drink tea and talk about music or books. That's it—a fantasy of intellectual contact, of voices talking. Unlike real life or memory, fantasies retain a fixed specificity, layers of details building into a repeatable drama that, hopefully, doesn't become absurd.

This Beatles fantasy is one of refuge in that John or Paul comes to me out of a need for simplicity, my ability to offer the ordinary to two extraordinary men. This fantasy is the antithesis of glamour. I'm not being swept away by a handsome star; instead, the handsome star comes sweeping into my house because he needs to unload his glamour. *Cup of tea, John?* And I didn't even know the proper way to make a pot until Ian taught me how. Ah, memories.

Even in the dark I knew it was Ian, his greatcoat opening behind him as he walked down the middle of the traffic island. "Stop," I yelled at Ruth, who was driving. "Let me out, I'll see you later," I commanded as she braked.

"It's you, is it?" he said, as I bounded toward him. I wasn't yet used to his submerged responses, the French shrug, the half-smile-half-smirk. If he was surprised, he hid it well, a master of deflection.

"Who else?" I countered. "Tis I."

"Tis indeed."

Who could/would tolerate such dialogue, even if, decades later, it's not verbatim? It's close enough. I had met Ian at Ruth's party, and then, some months later, in the middle of traffic, I met him again.

A party from forty years ago. It was summer, Washington, DC, in the early 1980s. Ruth lived on the top floor of a house with a staircase that brought you into a hallway. I remember looking down that staircase as three people were coming up. One was Gary, a mysterious man who was seemingly irresistible to every woman he met, including, at different times, Ruth and me. Behind him was a lovely, tall blonde woman who, I learned that night, was Ian's wife, and behind her was Ian, looking a bit like Richard Burton, but younger, thinner, and with a plop of bangs. Oh, those blue, blue eyes. He resembled the man in that photograph I had razored out of a library book during my Beatles mania, circa 1964—*The man in the pub,* handsome, aloof, leaning back against wood paneling, a half-pint on the table in front of him. And here he was, climbing toward me.

What was he wearing? A checked shirt, dark trousers, tennis shoes? Not a neat dresser, just a good talker. Someone must have told him I was in graduate school studying literature, for how else did we end up in Ruth's kitchen arguing about Edna O'Brien for hours?

"Oh, that slut," he announced, and we were off.

Ian is Scottish for John.

Back in those days I often argued about literature with people, even strangers. I liked standing my ground and maybe learning something from them in the process. I'd argue about music, too, but I don't remember Ian and me drawing swords over Beatles versus Stones at the party. If not then, then soon enough. Seeing him on the traffic island was serendipitous; soon after that, we met more often.

I was taken with Ian's good looks, his accent, the Elizabethan sweep of his coat, but what did I really know about him? He grew up in Kent, never went to university but was quite well-read and astute. He had a "living," but I never knew exactly what that meant. In passing, he mentioned the horrors of English boarding schools. He didn't seem materialistic, dressed inattentively, smoked too much and had a small mouth. He was married to an American woman, they had two children, and more would come. He was both rude and gallant in a very British way, and one time I witnessed a man who knew Ian verbally humiliate him while we sat at a bar having a drink. He liked to put down intelligent women but needed to be surrounded by them. He'd read all of Trollope, he danced more with his elbows than with his feet, and he thought nothing of appearing unannounced on my doorstep at eleven p.m. I always let him in.

We had what I'd describe as a *salon a deux*: we talked and talked and talked, sometimes in the car, sometimes while lying on my bed, sometimes in his apartment, sometimes while watching naked women dance at the local tittie bar. Some necessity had entered our lives, and neither of us seemed in any hurry to be without it.

We were never lovers, never kissed or cuddled. Instead, our meetings carried a negatively charged sexual vibe, as though we each knew we'd disappoint the other if we ever did become physical. Because neither of us was keen on adultery, this knowledge served as a kind of relief, one that allowed us to inhabit sexual environments worry-free. This in itself created a weird kind of romance, one that despite our abstinence, was very sexy, or at least sexy to me.

I expect I offered refuge to Ian, one where our respective real-life concerns didn't dissipate but were momentarily suspended. I believe he was homesick for England, and all the questions I asked about his upbringing, schooling, and country either made that worse or helped mitigate it; I'll never know.

His Englishness helped minimize my American loneliness, and his unpredictable arrivals brought zest to my routine domestic life. I was a single mom, and he was a husband and father trying to settle into a new country and system of work. The last thing either of us wanted to talk about was domestic issues. It felt luxurious to stay up late trying to outsmart each other. I was queen of the outlandish pronouncement, the ramped-up metaphor, his response a smirk quickly defused by a smile, and sometimes genuine disbelief, but we managed to stay on topic or make the leap to another one. He was the only man I discussed the Beatles with who didn't initially ask me, *Did you scream?* He once asserted that John Lennon's politics were naïve but quickly appended that by saying *At least Lennon was sincere in his naiveté.* I've come to agree with him about that. So much of our conversation depended on irony and sarcasm, but removing them might have revealed an intimacy that wasn't there, or one we couldn't possibly sustain given his marriage. There was no definite break, but over time our friendship faded, as many friendships do.

For years I've had dreams about Ian, all of which seem to take place in a variety of rooms seething with suspense. I've had dreams about his wife as well. These dreams must represent something to me, a long marriage for sure, one with many children, something I'll never have. But there must be more to it than that. Could the dreams represent my guilt surfacing after all these years? If not the "other" woman, I was certainly "an other" woman, disruptive to Ian's household, even though I was considered a family friend, a sometimes babysitter, and a helpful resource. At the time, I refused to see my complicity from his wife's perspective because I was practicing a selective feminism: I wanted to believe it was possible to be friends with her husband at eleven o'clock at night. Even talk carries a price, one that, at the time, I refused to consider.

One afternoon at my house, with March blowing and the trees greening outside, Ian taught me how to make a proper pot of tea. He explained the necessities: heat, sugar, milk, the importance of listening to the water heating, to read its hiss and then the quick splash into the teapot, a quick swish out, and then the tea bags dropped into the final water. "Now comes the hardest part," he said.

There we stood at my kitchen counter, one untraveled American, one homesick Englishman, looking at a brown ceramic teapot. "So what's the hardest part?" I asked. Ian answered, "Waiting."

In 1985, Ian taught me how to make tea. In 1986, I traveled to England. My plan was to see Liverpool and meet as many Englishmen as I could.

PLUMTREE COURT LAWYER

He knew I was American the minute he saw me sitting all by my lonely in a London pub. He came with me back to my B & B; we climbed four sets of stairs. I pleasured him, he turned away, I said, "How about you helping me?" He said, "No, I'm flying to Italy tomorrow with my fiancée." An honest bloke, he knew the way out. End of story, and such a predictable one.

But not completely. A few days after I returned home to America, he called to ask, "How are you doing, you OK?" his voice dripping with concern. I was rather surprised. Perhaps he thought he had damaged me, that London pricks (and I mean this in the fullest sense of the term) are more damaging than American ones, but no, it was his way of apologizing for the bluster and privilege he demonstrated in my rented room without mentioning either. When he called again some weeks later, I was touched. He said he might have to do some work in New York, which would mean a hotel room with a private bath. "Great," I said; then, "When's the wedding?" "In January, coming up." He never called again.

Plumtree Court. Such a romantic name. I've forgotten his.

THE SCOTTISH HEIR

Breakfast in the dining room of my London B & B, silver pots of tea every few inches on the rows of tables, a metallic silence—no one talking except the American husbands and wives, to each other. I don't recall saying a word, but I must have, because the young man who sat across from me two breakfasts in a row would have me for dessert soon enough.

My first lay in England. He was twenty at the most, clean-cut, nice looking. He worked for the Seagram family; perhaps, he hinted, was even an heir, which would make him more Scot than English, and more Canadian than both. Whatever. His room was as narrow as mine but had a window that faced the square. Summer evenings in England take their time. We got down to it.

He was awed, positively awed, at my brashness, my trash talk, and attempted to give it right back with his own combination of north-of-the-wall slang and Old Testament chest thumping. After he told me I was *a wicked, shameful harlot, nothing but a hussy redheaded hoor he'd like to turn over to his brothers when they returned from a full day of haying,* I immediately ascertained he was an avid churchgoer and, when not selling gin in London, vacationed in the Highlands.

How else to explain that he'd *fair puckle me until I became foosty and totally maist cuntit,* that he could tell I was a *twally washer with a big bahooky* and two nice coconuts. There was no *beweeping* for us, he was too busy spouting, though I had a hunch I was the first female he'd tried out such lines on. Poor lamb.

I wasn't scared; I was having a ball, watching him hold his own, as only young men can when they concentrate so hard on not coming they age decades before your eyes. When that happens, you call upon your inner third-grade teacher during a fire drill: "Hurry along, now, that's a good boy . . . ," and it turned out he *was* a good boy.

We got dressed and sat in Russell Square watching the evening birds. I have no memory of what we said. Then we went back to his room for more Bible study, fooking and foostying.

Thirty years on, he emails me. He found my scholarly work listed somewhere and wrote to tell me he remembered our discussing Hemingway. When could that literary conversation have taken place, considering all our puckling? But I believed him. Then I hit delete.

ST. IVES SCHOOLTEACHER, MILKMAN, AND MAN ON THE TRAIN

I ventured to St. Ives, took the little red wooden train around the cliffs down to the central square, gathered my bags and climbed a steep hill to another B & B. I was wearing the long raincoat I bought at Banana Republic for drizzly seaside days, and everywhere I went I noticed a tall man wearing a blue windbreaker. I could tell that he noticed me, too, and when we both rushed to get beneath an awning and out of a sudden shower, he introduced himself. I've forgotten his name, but not what he did or where he lived: taught school in Croydon. This made an impression because Croy is my maiden name. Later I learned that D. H. Lawrence once taught school in Croydon and hated every minute of it.

My Croydon man took me to dinner and introduced me to single malt Scotch. Seagulls flew outside the restaurant's window in big silvery swoops. There would be no swooping between us, however, though I tried hard to work some up. Back then, one bloke in every port of call was my travel itinerary, thinking it a fine way to get to know the English. So far a lawyer, a distiller, a teacher—well, you can't win 'em all.

Walking solo back to my B & B, I realized that traveling made me lonely, and that I was getting tired. Perhaps the next night in St. Ives would be better, and it was: I met a milkman and his wife, and while shooting pool we talked about John Lennon and Bob Dylan. Here was an Englishman who didn't spend much time thinking about the Beatles but admitted to having a shrine in his house to Bob. "Aye, he does at that," his wife confirmed.

In America in 1986, a young man might have found delivering milk for a living embarrassing, but this St. Ives milkman was proud—"That's what my dad does, too." There had been only politeness and small talk between me and the schoolteacher, not much to build a lasting memory on. But I will always remember the St. Ives milkman, the young rock and roller who asks for nothing but steady work and beer on the weekends. He told me that listening to Dylan sing "The Ballad of a Thin Man" made his life worthwhile. A true fan.

After leaving St. Ives on the little red train, I waited for my connection outside the St. Erth station. When the train arrived, I stepped into what I thought was an empty car but soon realized there was another person sitting at the front. Just the two of us.

He was a slight man, a bit greasy, black beneath his nails. He'd been camping at St. Agnes and was on his way to another campsite. Turned out he was a bricklayer, but the discussion soon switched to literature. What a revelation!

This man with rough hands who had left school at fourteen could tell you more about the English novel than many graduate students I knew. If I wanted to understand England in the twentieth century, he suggested I read *The Ragged Trousered Philanthropists* by Robert Tressell, a 1914 novel I'd never heard of, though some consider it the best socialist novel ever written. When I returned to London, I bought a copy at Dillons, the bookstore where I also bought a copy of Hemingway's *The Sun Also Rises* published under its British title, *Fiesta*. My bricklayer forgot to tell me Tressell's novel was over a thousand pages long, and I gave it my best, but in the end I gave up and passed it along to one of my professors who was excited to receive it.

THE SHORT MEN OF LIVERPOOL

After leaving St. Ives for Liverpool, I noticed something: the farther north I went, the shorter the men. My Croydon teacher was over six foot. My Plumtree lawyer was big and strapping. Seagrams was also tall. But the St. Ives milkman wasn't, nor was the bricklayer on the train. By the time I got to Liverpool, I began to see not only Ringo Starr in a new light, but Gerry Mardsen of the Pacemakers, Billy J. Kramer, and Eric Burden, all short men. Liverpool men who weren't musicians had another talent: talking.

As soon as I stepped off the train and walked through Lime Street Station, I was spoken to, nodded at, eyed with genial interest and made to feel included. In one crowded bar, a gesture-friendly young man, five-six at the most, could have been Hennie Youngman's son, he had so many one-liners, many directed at my being American, and everyone within earshot roared with laughter, including me. My waiter at dinner, also short, said something funny every time he came to my table. The pudgy cab driver who drove me past the Cavern Club and the docks kept up a breathless soliloquy concerning his hometown but frequently returned to another, more personal subject: *I can show you what a real Liverpool man is like if you wish, luv, but ya gotta wait until me shift is done then I'll drive you for free if you want, what say you, luv, game or no?* Each time he spoke his neck would swivel toward me, but he sat so low in his seat I could hardly make out his face.

So there I was, in the backseat of a cab contemplating a charity fuck for no good reason other than I was in the city of my dreams and, what the hell, why not have a knee wobbler up against some grimy Victorian pile? But I was so tired, so cash-poor, and the realization that I had stupidly planned my trip backward began to sink in as the cab took one turn after another through the dark streets.

Why hadn't I begun my trip in Liverpool? Why had I spent so much time in St. Ives, or even visited Exeter? Why hadn't I realized that Oxford University was closed before I went there for a day of lonely walking and a Belgian waffle at the train station? My Liverpool cabbie was rambling on when suddenly he stopped. *"You OK, luv? I'm just larking, you know, take you back to your hotel now, luv?"* *"No, not yet, it's just that I'm tired and don't know where I am. What should I see, do you think? I don't want to be a tourist."* He was quiet for a bit, then he said, *"One more stop then back to the Lord Nelson, I'll show you the real Liverpool, luv, I'll show you."*

His real Liverpool was a brightly lit bar at closing time, low class but calm, full of both old and young people, all of them friendly drunk. A circle had formed in the middle of the room and we joined it. Then there was a bit of commotion, some yelling and urging on, and someone with a bucket stepped into the circle and began throwing sawdust on the floor. More yells, a bit of shoving, then an old, almost toothless man in dirty clothes appeared and stood before us. He looked around, rubbed his hands together and began to dance. Everyone began to sing and clap as the old man danced his jig. It couldn't have lasted for more than a minute. The circle broke up and the cabbie took me back to my hotel. *"Good night, luv, you're a pretty redhead American, I hope I didn't offend you."* No, he hadn't offended me; he showed me the real Liverpool, even if to this day I'm not sure what exactly I really saw.

MY MICHAEL CAINE LOOK-ALIKE

After the long train ride from Liverpool back to London, I was lucky to get a room in a white stucco hotel on a block full of white stucco hotels. I didn't want to end up like a Jean Rhys character, roomless and walking the streets hoping someone would buy her a brandy. I had one more day and night in London before I flew home.

I strolled around and bought some books and, for my teenage daughter, a pair of white fishnet fingerless gloves. I had come to terms with my poor trip planning, telling myself that there'd always be a Liverpool, and that at least I had been there, however briefly, however nocturnally. I had a deep aversion to being seen as just another Beatles fan and loathed the idea of taking a gawk at Penny Lane from the Magical Mystery Tour Bus, a vehicle that cruised the streets like a lumbering harlot dressed up in more colors than an acid trip. I appreciated my cabbie's candor when he told me, as we drove past the Cavern Club, *That's not the original one, luv, that one we tore down over ten years back. This one here is the new Cavern Club.* Even if I returned with more time and money, would I see any of the original Liverpool? Is there any left?

In 2009, Bob Dylan joined a tour of Mendips, Aunt Mimi's house where John grew up and which is now part of the National Trust. Dylan wanted to sit in John's bedroom and look out its window. He longed for a private experience between the living and the dead in which a part of the past is shared in the present. Dylan's 2012 album, *Tempest,* ends with "Roll on John," a tribute song to the boy whose musical dreams began in that narrow room with one window.

Dylan's experience, undoubtedly fine-tuned in recognition of his celebrity, is the opposite of other popular Liverpool tours, which are filled with mop-top-look-alikes, faux memorabilia, reconstituted venues, the full high-gloss treatment that ensures the complete Disneyfication of J, P, G & R. This was inevitable, of course, given how the fame industry functions. But before John's death in 1980, Liverpool didn't want much to do with the Beatles, as many felt the boys had abandoned their hometown. Yet fans and other locals prevailed, and now Beatles memory tours are citywide and fuel Liverpool's economy. One company that's doing well is the Fab4CabTour. *Hello, Luv.*

After shopping, I returned to my London hotel, where Michael Caine was waiting for me. Or at least his facsimile— a pack of ciggies on the bar, black-frame glasses, and crooked teeth. Charming, forthright and fun, a sales representative, if I remember correctly, who detrained at Marylebone Station every few weeks to do business in London. We would never meet again, I knew that. In a week I'd be mowing my summer lawn and putting out the trash, but on my last night in London I experienced local joys.

This time it was my room, a yellow square of tiled walls, the dying sunshine coming through a high window. I remember calling our lovemaking "a lovely soup"—constant motion, constant moisture, his face above me constantly smiling. No script to follow, no recriminations, just a mutually, wonderfully friendly, uncomplicated screw. I left London tired but happy.

On a hot day some weeks later, I was resting on my stoop looking through the mail. My Michael Caine had sent me a letter along with a photograph: he was naked in a shower stall, holding the see-through curtain coyly across his groin with one hand while the other was raised above his head as though waving. He was wearing his black-frame glasses and had a big smile on his face. I squinted and looked closer. Yes, he reminded me of Michael Caine, but those glasses, that maniacal smile—they were part Lennon, too.

IT'S ONLY LOVE

John Lennon once characterized the lyrics of his song "It's Only Love" as "abysmal," and though I think few would agree with him (the song is a lovely little thing), his comment does suggest the shortcomings of depending on language to define such a complex endeavor as love.

Words can't solve the problems we have with love, but they can give us choices, even if, sometimes, the words themselves are the problem. For example, how should we understand the word "only"? When John sings "it's only love," is he being flippant or ironic? Or does the "only" represent something conditional and unsaid, such as it's only love if you pay the rent and promise to sell your Danny Osmond albums?

And what *is* love? Like a gun in the hands of a blind four-year-old, love is liable to go off in many directions before it hits its mark, if it ever does. Tough love? A vaunted oxymoron. Sexual love? Great while you have it, but when it ends it sometimes leads to homicide. Unconditional love? It might exist, pulsing in some miles-deep ocean crevice, oozing up from time to time to the upper levels of life. But to practice it you have to ignore all you know about human nature, including the dark thoughts you had last week about your own two-year-old. Marital love? Sought after but, unfortunately, not foolproof and too rarely achieved.

If Cynthia Lennon were to weigh in on the matter, what would be her "only," her "love"? Could you, would you love this person: *He was a pill-popping drunk, a self-proclaimed hitter of women who was chronically unfaithful to his wife, who did emotional injury to his first son, who made fun of the disabled and called a man who loved him a "Jew fag" to his face. He is reputed to have stolen records from his friends, once brutally stomped a man at a party, consorted with whores and groupies, drove without his glasses or a license, boasted of having taken 1,000 LSD trips, dreamed of having sex with his mother; a man who sniffed heroin, who puked in public, who thought himself a genius and always had from the age of ten, who drew obscene pictures, who posed nude, who didn't wash his hair or give his wife a generous divorce settlement, a man with an acid tongue, a plagiarist, a musician who constantly dropped his notes, a man who gave his autograph to his own assassin.*

Or could you, would you, love this person? *He bought his Aunt Mimi a house, another for his half-sisters, gave thousands to his childhood friend to start a business. He worked for peace. He was sentimental, generous, funny, lost, and alone. He made music out of this. He broke hearts; he tried to know his own. A hoarder of memories and objects from the past, he kept his childhood drawings, the wacky little stories he wrote. He openly loved a woman others hated. He slept on the floor of her hospital room in case she bled out during her pregnancy. He grew up among a matriarchy of aunties—talc, hankies, water hissing on the coil. He wore short pants. He learned to bake bread. He read the newspapers faithfully. He had an incredible smile, like a flash of otherworldly light directed your way. "It's just me, Paul," he once said, lowering his glasses. Millions of dollars were on the table, but love was not enough.*

Cynthia loved this man, and I love him, too. Because love is the grandest human emotion, it requires the grandest of human rationalizations. Although John behaved badly, I love him because he's powerful, real, and talented. We all love according to our own although/because dyad, but the balancing of these rationalizations is probably different for everyone, perhaps even coming down to a matter of taste. I'm pretty certain I could never love someone who admired Donny Osmond.

Once John began taking LSD, Cynthia's "although" outweighed her "because." Even then it still took discovering Yoko Ono sitting in Cynthia's kitchen wearing Cynthia's housecoat for Cynthia to make her move. Cynthia was no Hillary Clinton, who has the public ability to overlook deceits her husband Bill enacted in private. When John's indiscretion went public, Cynthia acted to protect herself and her son by finally asking for a divorce. We shouldn't fault her for waiting as long as she did. Hera never divorced Zeus, either.

At the end of her memoir *John,* Cynthia writes that she will always love him, but if she had known earlier what he would put her through she never would have married him; in fact, she would have run away the first time she saw him. These are strong words, ones when scrutinized don't make a lot of sense. Can you always love a person you wish you'd never met? Cynthia is not being disingenuous; she's describing the mystery of love and the confusion it causes. Love is the Rolls Royce of negative capability. You ride in it until something really bad happens, like finding Yoko in your kitchen. Until then, to exist in uncertainty is one of love's principal characteristics.

Unlike Cynthia, who knew John was taking LSD for quite some time, I didn't know that my boyfriend Lucas was taking hard drugs. When the sheets we slept on turned brown with his sweat, I thought he might have TB. His father died of TB, not an uncommon death for a poor black man in the mid-1950s, and I thought the disease might have been dormant in Lucas for twenty years. Silly me.

When Lucas began buying capsules of vitamin E for his skin, I thought it was a black thing; he'd get ashy and rub stuff on his elbows and shins. After I got suspicious that something awful might be going on, I began picking through the trashcan in our basement bathroom. I wasn't sure what I was looking for, a needle, perhaps, some absolute visual proof. Instead, I found little broken tubes wrapped in what looked like tin foil and tied off at both ends. Amyl nitrite poppers. When I found out what they were, I wondered if Lucas was hanging out at gay discos. There were lots of whirling silver balls dangling from DC ceilings during the mid-1970s. Then there was the evening his cousin blocked my way into the kitchen because Lucas had puked on the floor, *some bad Chinese*, he told me, and I took his word for it.

They say love is blind, but the afternoon I forced up the sleeve of Lucas's shirt and saw the raised ropes of needle tracks, I knew what I was looking at: the end of our love, perhaps one that had been doomed from the beginning given all the social differences it included. Nevertheless, it was a grand love.

Five years after we split, Lucas OD'd. His oldest sister called to tell me he was in the hospital. The first time I visited, Lucas was in a coma, lying naked on the bed with only a white napkin covering his genitals. Multiple tubes had been inserted into his body, and country and western music was playing on the radio. Could he even hear it, or hear me? I told him I'd turn the radio to a soul station, but it was too high on the shelf for me to reach. Two days later I visited again. This time he was in a different room, and all the tubes had been removed. Later that night he died.

We love although. We love against. We love in spite of. We love when we know it will end. We love in order to save, and we're surprised when we are the ones who are saved. Lucas saved me. Coming off an abusive affair that almost destroyed my self-worth, feeling partly responsible for my mother's death because of the turmoil she suffered during the custody battle for my daughter, and navigating the difficulties of single motherhood, I was surprised when a pimp-strutting, Afro-haired, Kool-smoking brother who worked in the mailroom of a national organization turned out to be the man who would resurrect my sense of self and improve me in numerous ways. Very soon my surprise turned into gratitude.

For me, Lucas was not the complete antidote that Yoko was for John. John saw Yoko as himself, another artist; together they were the "two gurus in drag" from his famous song. She screamed, he screamed, and the rest is a great twentieth-century love story. Lucas and I did not merge into one entity so much as bounce off each other in convivial ways.

Racism impacted John and Yoko's union, but it did not define it, as it did mine and Lucas's. In 1975, taboos regarding mixed-race romances were still in place, though they had begun to loosen. Lucas gained ghetto status for having a white woman, and in return I got protected entry into the ghetto. It was a full education, one unavailable to me under any other circumstance. But it was also a painful one because learning about race in America means learning you're never permitted to forget it.

Lucas healed me sexually. He loved what he called my "freaky" self. He loved my full body and lavished it with attention every chance he got and everywhere he could. I learned how to give myself without fear of being criticized or shamed. In fact, Lucas released me from shame. He taught me to feel powerful.

The sad irony of all this ego boosting is that it didn't work in reverse. I learned very quickly what he had learned at birth: that an uneducated black man, however skilled at his job, had no security or real safety in the world, nor could he ever escape the casual racism that even children were capable of: when Lucas came down to breakfast the morning after a sleepover my eight-year-old daughter hosted, one of her friends, an Asian girl, pronounced, "Who's the black boy?"

Our dyad was sexual/social. We were fine in the former, fine, too, in the private moments of our friendship, which often involved hanging out with my father, but the social wouldn't leave us alone.

When Lucas lost his job, his world fell apart, and so did ours. That's when he began to take drugs (or at least that's when I discovered it), and that's when he began to lie. So I put him out, dropped off huge green trash bags stuffed with his belongings at the apartment of one of his sisters who lived in the city. No one in his family thought poorly of me for doing this. To them, Lucas had had a good thing with me, and he blew it. That was nice to hear, but it didn't prepare me for what else I heard that afternoon.

His sister told me Lucas had served years in prison for killing a man during a teenage act of retribution against the man who had tried to rape one of his sisters. Lucas and some other boys went after the molester with a baseball bat. While in prison, Lucas developed a reputation as a tough man, but his sister didn't explain what that meant and I didn't ask; she just gave me a steady, chilling look.

That afternoon, driving back to my nice suburban house, I took refuge in language. Though shocked, I didn't shun the facts of Lucas's past, but I did rearrange them to fit my needs. Lucas wasn't a killer; Lucas was a man who had killed. That's a distinction in and of itself, but it's especially a distinction love allows us to make, one families of military men make every day, though I do acknowledge killing in war is different from a neighborhood takedown.

Like Cynthia Lennon reflecting on John, had I known that Lucas had killed a man or had served time, I never would have become involved with him. Also, my knowing about Lucas's past might have reinforced in me the racial profile I grew up with, despite its being one my family didn't personally hold: black men were violent and criminal. Move on, don't look, cross back over the tracks. How does love stack up against such possible truths and pressures? With great difficulty, I think.

Though Lucas was out of my house, I still saw him from time to time. He depended on me for certain things, the simple act of *conversating,* as he called it, for one. I wonder if in his entire life Lucas ever had anyone who actually listened to him? He talked openly but vaguely to me about prison, but what he said made a lasting impression. *Two things about being in prison,* he told me: *it's never quiet and the lights are always on. Another thing about prison: every day you wake up, the first thing you think is, Is this the day I get killed or is this the day I'll have to kill someone?* It became clear to me that Lucas had probably asked that question every day of his life, even on those happy mornings he woke up next to me.

I could love Lucas only so much and for only so long. Can we only love if we lie? Does the truth make love insufficient? The social facts of Lucas, his race, his history, the great sadness I feel when I think of his lifelong pain, tell me this is so. Despite all that he gave to me, all he taught me, I could not sustain loving him. Violence had done its lasting damage.

And it's violence I keep returning to when I think about my love of John Lennon. While doing research for these essays, I was sickened to learn that some think John might have caused ex-Beatle Stu Sutcliffe's death by kicking him in the head. If true . . . well, it's probably not true, as the assertion was first made in Albert Goldman's scurrilous 1988 biography before it was taken up by Stu's sister, Pauline, when she began auctioning off her dead brother's paintings.

According to Goldman's biography, actually a "pathography," to use a word coined by Joyce Carol Oates, Lennon is also purported to have killed a sailor in Hamburg; to have kicked Yoko, causing her to miscarry; and to have supposedly frequented boy prostitutes in Thailand. Against these speculations, the one verified attack John did commit, the 1963 beating of Liverpool deejay Bob Wooler, which landed Wooler in the hospital, seems kid's stuff. After he attacked Wooler, John sank to his knees, weeping and wailing, *What have I done, what have I done,* vowing never to be violent again. According to Cynthia, who witnessed the attack, he never was.

Cynthia's memoir is difficult reading if one is looking for reasons to love John Lennon. She knew and loved John for over half his life, but love, loyalty, and family were insufficient. John's drug use, infidelities, verbal abuse, and emotional distance, especially to son Julian, all of which were compounded by the carceral conditions of his life brought about by worldwide fame, became overwhelming. Her memoir begins with her describing him as "infuriating, lovable, sometimes cruel, funny, talented and needy." It ends describing John as a "creative genius who sang movingly about love while often wounding those closest to him." In between these two quotes, the book is a rhapsody of because/although situations as steady and repetitive as a heartbeat. Cynthia, who herself was overwhelmed, could not have saved him from the despair his life had become.

It's possible, too, that John never loved Cynthia, given how difficult it is, even under the best of conditions, to determine what love really is. Like many of us, they "had to get married," pregnancy being the paramount condition that creates an often irremediable although/because conundrum. In 1962, he "did the right thing," and during the early years of Beatlemania, John depended on Cynthia for stability and encouragement. But that was not enough. John and Cynthia married under social pressures neither created, and when those pressures intensified, their marriage ended.

♪

"It's Only Love" initially appeared on the UK *Help!* album the summer of 1965. But it was not included on the American version of the album. Consequently, I didn't hear the song until Capitol released its stateside *Rubber Soul* in December 1965. On the UK *Help!*, the song is positioned between Ringo's twangy "Act Naturally" and George's sardonic "You Like Me Too Much." In this placement, "It's Only Love" sounds like the trifle John believed it was. Running just under two minutes, the song is mismatched with others on the album, most of which speak negatively about love. But heard on my *Rubber Soul* album, where it's positioned between Paul's wistful "Michelle" and John's tremulous "Girl," it shines.

Rubber Soul is credited with being the Beatles' first adult album, and on both the UK and the American versions, its songs are musically and thematically a leap forward from earlier pop song platitudes. The Beatles sing love songs full of mystery, longing, and even belligerence. The lyrics to "It's Only Love" teeter between the usual "sighs" and "butterflies" of generic songs, but the singer's uncertainty and mention of lovers fighting edge the song toward the real, concluding with this sad truth: *"It's so hard loving you."*

Framed within John and Cynthia's marriage, "It's Only Love" can be seen as confessional, though not in the way "Nowhere Man" or "Help!" is. Those two songs are stringent self-assessments, while "It's Only Love" reflects confusion. However, confusion can lead to clarity, and it's possible to see "It's Only Love" as a transitional song leading to later Lennon songs whose lyrics are full, forthright expressions of love, pain, and self-incrimination. I'm thinking of songs like "Oh My Love," "Julia," and "Jealous Guy," songs without irony, confusion, or self-consciousness, ones John would never have written had he not met Yoko Ono and fallen in love with her.

Adhering to neither mainstream social nor artistic pressures, Yoko provided John a new place in which to love and to create. But this place was not trouble free. Cynthia was yelled at and sometimes surrounded by jealous fans on the street, but she was always considered "one of us," a white English woman, something Yoko was not and never would be. The British press wasted no time reminding Yoko of her outsider status. She was referred to in the press as "Jap," "Chink," "yellow," and in one publication "Okay Yoni." On meeting Yoko, Aunt Mimi was horrified and asked, "Who's the poisoned dwarf, John?" On one occasion, some Beatles fans presented Yoko with a bunch of yellow roses, thorny stems first, and her hair was often pulled when she was out in public.

To this day, some still believe she broke up the Beatles, though evidence of their demise predates her arrival. At the minimum, she's been seen as a gold digger, at the maximum, a witch. Their nude photo on the cover of the album *Two Virgins* caused outrage but mainly snide comments about both their bodies, especially Yoko's droopy breasts. But the photos Annie Leibovitz took of John and Yoko in 1970 and then ten years later on the afternoon of December 8, the day John was murdered, attest to Yoko's beauty and to John's loving devotion.

In today's cynical media-intensive world, we should remember that John frequently defended Yoko in every available medium: print, television, interviews, and song. If we find his sincerity suspect, perhaps it's because such simple statements as his declaration "You see, we fell in love" are seldom heard from today's celebrities. Instead, they just upload a sex tape and hope for millions of tweets.

Yoko saved John Lennon. He had built a new life with her and their son Sean, but on the evening of December 8, 1980, Mark David Chapman's bullets cancelled that new life. John's bleeding body was shuttled into one police car while Yoko followed in another. It's said that the sense of hearing is the last to go, and that people in a coma or in the process of dying can still hear. That's why I tried to change the radio station when Lucas lay dying in his hospital bed. But when John was bleeding out in the backseat of that police car, it wasn't Yoko's voice he heard saying she'd change the channel on the radio but someone else's, and it was saying something awful.

AUGUST 14, 1965

A Day in My Life

Scottish singer Al Stewart knows a thing or two about the difficulty of meeting up with old friends. In the title cut of Stewart's 1975 album *Modern Times,* a chance meeting between two old school chums doesn't play out as we might like. One friend wants to reminisce, the other one doesn't want to remember. OK, but what if you *can't* remember? Are there songs for that?

Perhaps this is why I'm reluctant to contact my old friend Betty, she of the *bbbbBBs,* the Michael Landon crush, the Paul girl who fifty-five years ago sat next to me in Ed Sullivan's studio and watched the Beatles play. Fifty-five years are a lot of years.

I have a phone number that leads to an answering machine. I also have a number for her daughter, but there's no assurance either number will get me anywhere. I don't want to be the pest who inserts her needs into someone else's life, someone who might want to be left alone like Al Stewart's once-upon-a-time buddy. But another Scot, my unflappable friend Fiona, a journalist with boots-on-the-ground experience in London and in Northern Ireland, advises me to plunge on, to turn over all rocks and *get the girl's number and call her for ass sake.* Al Stewart offers me caution while Fiona offers me agency, and her admonishment tells me she's as curious as I am about my old friend. Betty, after all, is part of my life's story.

So, in the name of friendship, past and present, I will make a phone call. If I don't, August 14, 1965, a seminal day in the life of Sylvia "Sibbie" Croy O'Sullivan, might remain incomplete, hazy, and open to incomplete memories more than it already is. I was in search of verification.

I used to tell my creative writing classes that I had slept with John Lennon. No one ever questioned my assertion, and it certainly got their attention. My statement was a little lesson about writing, and it worked: make your audience believe you. Now this lesson is useless: I don't want to fabricate anything about August 14, 1965; I want to remember it. Unfortunately, there's very little of that day I do remember, and this lack of memory makes me a traitor to my own experience.

Before Betty and her parents picked me up for the ride to New York City, my mother slipped me a tenner. At the time, I hadn't realized how generous she was. In our household, ten dollars was nothing to sneeze at, but I soon discovered it didn't buy you much in the Big Apple. We arrived on Friday, August 13th, and checked into a hotel. That evening we went to the NBC studios and saw the taping of *The Tonight Show* with Johnny Carson. The band was terrific. Led by trumpeter Doc Severinsen, it played for half an hour before Ed McMahon warmed up the crowd. Finally, the famous introduction: *Here's Johnny,* and emerging from between the curtains, there he was. The Googled archives of *The Tonight Show* indicate the guests were Ted Sorensen and Joan Rivers. Joan Rivers!!!! Did I see Joan Rivers? I've always admired her brashness and humor, but I have no memory of her walking across the stage or of her telling jokes. Research helps, but it also hurts. What else have I forgotten?

After the Carson show, we had dinner, and for fifty-five years I've remembered the name of the restaurant as the Red Coach Inn. Close, but no cigar. In 1965 there *was* a Red Coach Grill, part of the Howard Johnson's operation, located at 7 East 58th Street. I found a postcard of it on eBay and the interior looked familiar—lots of red, lots of wood—but it's east of 30 Rockefeller Center, where *The Tonight Show* was taped. Did we walk? Take a cab? Who knows? Wherever we ate, we were seated at a round table, and as I looked over the menu embarrassment set in: I had already spent some of the ten dollars my mother had given me, and the pork chop with applesauce that I ordered cost seven, so I came up short. Betty's parents kindly picked up the tab.

Why can I remember what I ate fifty-five years ago and not remember every detail of seeing the Beatles?

Betty's father had gotten tickets for the show's dress rehearsal, scheduled for 2:30 p.m. before a live audience of 700. Another performance before a different audience would be taped at 7:30 p.m. This taped performance was subsequently televised on Sullivan's Sunday evening show on September 12th. No tape of the dress rehearsal exists, but the September 12th show, along with all previous performances the Beatles did for Sullivan, is available on DVD.

When exactly did Betty and I enter the studio? I don't know, but I have a clear memory of seeing John on stage in his shirtsleeves playing the electric keyboard and talking over his shoulder to a man wearing headphones. This had to have been during a sound check. The Beatles Bible states that the band had some concerns about the sound system and wanted it corrected, so I'll take one point for my memory on this matter.

Something else sticks in my mind about the keyboard. It was perpendicular to the stage, and when John leaned over to play it, he kicked one leg out behind him like Jerry Lee Lewis. But I don't know if he did this during the sound check or during the dress rehearsal. In the televised show, the keyboard is not perpendicular to the audience but facing it, horizontal with the stage. Why can I remember John at the perpendicular keyboard but have no memory of his playing it while Paul sang "I'm Down" during the dress rehearsal?

In the photograph of John I took that day, he's wearing a suit, as they all did for the dress rehearsal. He's standing in front of what looks like a piece of drywall on casters, a very ad hoc stage set, one quite different from the set seen a month later on the televised show. In the photo, John is just standing holding his guitar, or he could be playing it; I can't tell. Obviously, I took advantage of this off moment to secretly whip out my Instamatic camera, and I'm sorry I didn't keep shooting. But I was probably worried my camera would be confiscated, and then I'd lose John altogether.

That day in Ed Sullivan's studio, Paul debuted "Yesterday." This in itself is a historical moment because the song had not yet been released in America, though it was included on the UK *Help!* album, which eight days before was released in Britain, on August 6th. I'm hesitant to write that I remember Paul singing "Yesterday" while an onstage string quartet played behind him; this memory, like others of that day, is quite obscure. A Google search tells me my memory is likely correct. According to Elliot Magaziner, a violinist with the CBS orchestra, he played on stage while Paul sang "Yesterday." The televised tape shows Paul alone on stage singing the song to string accompaniment. It's likely, then, that the accompaniment was recorded during the dress rehearsal that Betty and I saw. Lucky us—we heard the song before the rest of America did.

August 14, 1965, remains dazed and confused. I've lost all chronology of what I saw, and there isn't one detail I can pull out of my brain that helps establish a usable timeline. Worse, I can't even remember what I was feeling as I watched the Beatles, and all through my teen years I was an expert at *feeling*. I can still remember the evening I sat on the brick wall of my junior high school and watched as a huge, orange sun sank below the horizon. *There's a hole in the sky,* I said out loud, perhaps the first metaphor I knowingly made, and it felt thrilling, almost regal, like a christening bestowed from an unknown source. The entire world had opened up before me. But what I felt while watching John bang on the piano, or what his voice sounded like coming through Ed Sullivan's microphone, is out of reach. The loss of vocal memory is especially grating. Though there were screamers in the audience, they were rather subdued, something I attribute to the large number of parents sitting beside their daughters. We could hear the band, but I can't remember how it sounded.

Perhaps my brain was so paralyzed from actually seeing John that it didn't deposit my feelings in the neurological containers specifically created to hold them for retrieval. Because I didn't scream or toss about, perhaps my memories of the event were quickly absorbed and then buried to make room for other, subsequent memories. When you piss yourself, or scream and pull your hair, those bodily experiences *are* your feelings, ones that don't need names or metaphors. But I've always needed names and metaphors to substantiate my feelings; recall the word, recall the feeling, and then feel again through language. When feeling is forgotten, language becomes untrustworthy and the experience lives in exile until something releases it. I'm hoping my old friend Betty might be that something.

John called himself a "record man," meaning he preferred the repeatable experience of listening to a record as opposed to seeing the singer in concert. Compared to the evanescent nature of a live performance, a record is as solid as Stonehenge. The details of the performance I saw on Ed Sullivan's stage are forever lost between my twisty, age-dampened synapses. Even if they came rushing back, I'm not sure I could trust them because my memories of the August 14th live dress rehearsal are undoubtedly compromised by my viewing of the September 12th televised show, which I have watched many times on DVD. The camera chooses what viewers will see and, consequently, what they will remember. Since the August 14th camera filmed more of Paul than of John, my memories of seeing John live recede further into the unreachable part of my brain.

Confused and conflated—that's the sum total of my experience seeing the Beatles live. All I can do is hold on to what critic Mark Ford calls, in an essay on T. S. Eliot, "saturated fragments." However, time has diluted my fragments. Some still may have their "personal saturation value," something Eliot believed akin to memory, but shouldn't mine amount to more than a pork chop with a side of applesauce? There is no record of what I saw that day, and there never will be. All I have for sure is the geographic fact: *I was there.* This alone gives me and my memories, however incomplete, a status many other Beatles fans don't have. The only material proof of that status is my photograph of John. About twelve years ago, after decades of keeping it as a memento, I sold my ticket stub because I needed money. It's only paper, I remember thinking, what's paper compared to experience, to memories? But I will never sell my photograph of John.

Betty, old friend, you who used to ride me double on the back of your bike to the horse stables three miles uphill from where we lived, Betty, do you remember any of our day in New York City? Have I been hallucinating for fifty-five years? What did I see and hear, and why can't I remember it the way I remember myself, after all these years?

Your parents are dead, as are mine. But I remember the back of your mother's head above the front seat, your father, quiet as always, driving. Then something, a truck maybe, a mad swerve, your mother's pitched voice and my heart thumping, as it's done ever since when I'm in a car going over fifty. We were in the backseat, probably looking through magazines, pointing to photos, making funny noises. What's to look at on the New Jersey Turnpike? I was sixteen, you had just turned seventeen. When did we stop oozing? When did you take down your Beatles poster to make room for something else, something like the anatomy of a pig, or the parts of a horse, the animals you went on to study?

Betty, where are you? Couldn't you just drive by my house like you did that day twenty years ago, stopping the car when you saw me in my yard? So what if at first I wasn't sure who you were. People change, cars change. I was in the yard with The Man I Love, and as a joke I introduced him to you as Buzzy, a name I expected you would recognize from junior high school. I can remember the plaid shirt Buzzy used to wear, its autumn colors stretched tight across his chest. I also remember your father in his white underwear getting out of bed and dashing to the bathroom in the New York hotel room, that room with its two double beds. I'm sure we giggled. He used to call you Bets. But I can't remember Ringo singing "Act Naturally" on stage at Studio 50, though I know he did, because I've seen the tape.

All curiosity is selfish, and so is nostalgia: you want to know, you want to feel, you want to solidify experiences. But is this need universal? My impulse to pin down my *I was there* moments is the opposite of someone who's happy he or she is *no longer there*. Life is lived both backward and forward. Nevertheless, there's only one person responsible for my seeing the Beatles live on Ed Sullivan's stage fifty-five years ago: Betty, my old friend, who was there with me. I'd like to thank her. I've called her twice. Maybe she'll call me back, but maybe she won't.

BEAUTIFUL BOY/GIRL

It's just one photograph, but it breaks my heart every time I see it. John is sitting with his young son Julian, both flanked by two giant stuffed bears, a panda and a gray koala. By the looks of him, John is fully into his psychedelic habits and has a scary, penetrating gleam to his eyes, and Julian, poor Julian, looks as unhappy as any kid of four or five can look. Even the bears are scary—twice as big as Julian and unsmiling, threatening. This is no Alice in Wonderland frolic where the world is magically oversized and wacky. This is a photo of Julian's entrapment. Held in place by his dad and corralled by his stuffies, there's no way out.

I have two photographs of my then-four-year-old daughter that still hurt me. Both were taken during a preschool Halloween party. In one photo, nine children pose in their costumes and masks, and in the other they've removed their masks. Kim's mask, with its elongated smile and arched brows, is a cross between a clown and a princess. With the mask off, her face is sad and serious. I hate looking at this photograph because I know I'm the cause of her sadness, but the one where she wears the mask elicits a deeper pain because it suggests she's learned to hide that sadness.

Kids are notorious for not complimenting the camera with their best faces. Perhaps Julian was just up from his nap, or Kim was fighting that throat infection she had when she was four. But young children are also truth tellers or, better still, truth demonstrators. What they cannot know with their minds they articulate through their bodies and faces. Even Cynthia, Julian's mother, described her young son's face as having a "medieval quality to it, like carvings . . . on ancient gravestones."

Other photos of Julian are not as sad as this one. One has John and baby Julian sitting on the floor twirling a top. Photographs of Julian with Cynthia are, on the whole, much happier, but regardless of the loving adults present during his early years, including Paul McCartney, Julian carried in his face and body the same weight as my daughter: the weight of a family falling apart.

We so want our children to be happy that an unsmiling face can trigger a plethora of parental self-condemnations: I have failed; I'm selfish; what will the neighbors think; I don't love my child enough; and the most condemning: I'm a bad mother. Throughout my divorce and the high dudgeon of its subsequent custody battle, my capacity to be a "good" mother was the question upon which my daughter's future life and happiness rested.

Was John a good parent? Did he love Julian? You could ask the same of me regarding my daughter. I broke up our family, and because of that she would no longer have two parents living with her, the American ideal of a "good" family.

At four, Kim had her own suitcase, and I would watch from the door as her small, sturdy body carried it down the walk to where her father stood at the gate. Such obedience, such soldiering from one so young, such a straight back. She walked that distance between her mother and father, one that never lessened, for over ten years. Everyone got used to it, I suppose, but when Kim was little, I'd get teary watching her go. I also felt mean and sad: what was I was sending her away for? For the fifteen dollars a week of child support the court ordered her father to pay me? Yet I also felt relief and release. When she was with her father, I had time for myself and for adult endeavors. I would never have earned a PhD were it not for those weekends, nor would I have had time to write. Romance, too, if I was lucky. But many times I was alone, and often lonely. Like mother, like daughter, you might ask? Given my situation, I avoided making this comparison.

Like Cynthia, I got pregnant. It was 1970. I knew my life was about to change, but I didn't know the specifics. I doubt any childless woman does. While shopping for someone to marry us, Kim's father and I spoke with the local Unitarian minister, who advised I get an abortion, a procedure not yet fully legal in Maryland, though there was an allowance for "mental health cases." "I won't marry you," the minister said, "forced marriages never work, too much hanging over the two of you." He was right, but at the time I couldn't imagine getting an abortion. I'd never even had a pelvic exam, so I wasn't about to invite needles and instruments into my inner regions. And I was carrying a child, smaller than a grain of salt, yes, but one I'd already named. *Gazoony-Boony* I'd whisper to my belly every night, and as the pregnancy progressed, we'd have conversations. I loved and wanted this baby.

A few months later on my wedding day, I could no longer avoid what else was growing inside me: the knowledge I didn't want to spend my life with my baby's father. Over the next three years of marriage, I would suffer a series of epiphanies I could neither dismiss nor nudge into the future in hopes that time and habit would diminish them, beginning with the fact that my husband had a squeaky Donald Duck toy hidden in his pocket during our wedding. During the ceremony, he didn't squeak it, but I was worried he would. It wasn't a matter of love/don't love him; I didn't know what love was. But I did know he was the wrong man for me.

Something pulls women to men who have lost their fathers. When my husband was ten, his father died. What did you do? I asked him, trying to imagine how it felt to lose a parent so young. He told me he played with his toy cars in his grandfather's driveway on the day of his father's funeral, a funeral he wasn't allowed to attend. Immediately, an image of a lone boy playing in a driveway took hold of my mind with such force that it's never left. This image was my first experience with desolation, however removed and secondhand.

Perhaps it's desolation I see in Julian's face, for certainly he has lost his father many times over, first to constant work, then to drugs, divorce, and distance, and finally to death.

Historically, the system of patriarchy depended on the father providing for his family, controlling his wife and disciplining his sons to become fit inheritors of family property. There wasn't much emotion involved. The sentimental notion of fatherhood that began in the nineteenth century was generally applied to the bourgeoisie, but many working-class mothers rallied behind these new notions of parenting as a way to gain respectability for their families. D. H. Lawrence's 1910 novel *Sons and Lovers* scrambled that egg with astounding results.

In Liverpool, the performance of respectability also fueled the Stanley family. When Alf Lennon married Julia Stanley, her family was dismayed. When, upon Alf's desertion, Julia took up housekeeping with Bobby Dykins, Aunt Mimi took custody of John in order to raise him in a more respectable home. In Mimi's house, for the first time in his life, John had a daily father figure, Uncle George, Mimi's husband. Mimi insisted that John go to the best Liverpool schools, practice good manners, and dress appropriately, thus ensuring the future Beatle was raised properly. Uncle George supplied the comic relief to Aunt Mimi's severity. By all accounts, John and his uncle had a loving relationship. Unfortunately, Uncle

George died suddenly when John was fourteen. Like so many men I have known, John became fatherless.

In 1972, when my state, Maryland, passed its Equal Rights Amendment, the impact on family law was immediate: husbands could now contest alimony rulings, fathers could demand custody, and wives could finally sue their husbands for "criminal conversation"—you know, the kind that takes place between a husband and his neighbor's wife in the backseat of the Buick.

The amendment prohibited "all classifications based on sex," but, in custody trials, many judges still ruled according to the common law "maternal preference doctrine," unless the mother was deemed "unfit." In 1973, my husband set out to prove I was exactly that.

I wanted so desperately to get out of my marriage that I ignored my lawyer's advice and pled guilty to adultery. I was granted a divorce on the spot, a *vincula matrimonii*, which is not a designer pasta. At the time, there were few quick legal exits from a marriage; insanity and homicide were two others, so I really didn't have a choice when I pled adultery. Besides, my husband could easily prove I was unfaithful, so why not admit the truth. The truth would set me free, wouldn't it? At the time, I felt I was making a brave stand against the sexual double standard, and one for female equality.

I had also stupidly convinced myself that losing custody of Kim wouldn't be a disaster. Her father was not a bad man, and he loved her. We could have a modern arrangement, couldn't we, and I'd be free of the daily chores of childrearing, which I sometimes resented, and then perhaps I'd be able to take two night school classes at the university instead of one. I would be a liberated woman—they were all over the movies in the '70s. Still, every time I had these thoughts, I was crossing my fingers behind my back. I couldn't comprehend losing Kim, so I belittled what might happen if I did lose her. The task of facing that possible loss was too enormous, too uncomfortable; I simply refused to think about it.

So I coasted on blind faith, believing that after the interviews and house visits were over; after my husband, his friends, and his therapist had finished shaming me; after the social worker had called my mother "drab" and me "amoral"; after my then-lover laughingly testified he had no intention of marrying me; after my father turned to the judge and said, "No, your honor, my wife is not here. She passed away in March"; and after my lawyer shut his briefcase and straightened his tie, Kim would be mine. And, per the judge's ruling announcement, she was.

The ironies are evident, of course, especially in the way they upset the usual assumptions about gender. Here I was taking a stand against a sexual double standard men had devised and benefitted from, but it was men, my father and the judge, who really won Kim for me. After learning of my mother's death, the judge, in a moment of male bonding, leaned toward my father, who was on the stand, and extended his condolences. I have no doubt that the sympathy the judge felt for my recently widowed father weighed his decision in my favor.

But the real surprise was the female social worker. Somewhere in the bowels of the courthouse there is a transcript that spells out my ignominy. One day I will get a copy of that transcript and burn it. Both in her written report and in her testimony, this social worker pronounced me amoral, careless, selfish, and immature and chastised me for supposedly choosing my then-boyfriend over my daughter. Why couldn't I have both, I wondered?

She, a woman, probably a mother herself, would take my child from me because I had slept with another man. Is it any wonder then that I aligned myself with men, or that, at the height of feminist literary criticism, my academic area of study was men and masculinity, or that I distrusted most women, especially other mothers, lest they judge me as she had? I had secured my daughter, but I remained confused about who the enemy was: men or women?

Cynthia Lennon had the same confusion. When John threatened to take custody of Julian, Cynthia wondered if his cruel threat might have been Yoko's doing, given that Yoko herself did not have custody of her own daughter. Was it a matter, then, of *If I can't have mine, you can't have yours?* A bit of maternal *schadenfreude?* Deviousness, or in the case of my social worker, public shaming, has always been a female weapon. However, another possible source of Yoko's lack of generosity, if indeed that actually was the case, might be the absence of maternal love from her own mother. Young Yoko was raised by servants, not her parents.

In her searing, beautiful and sometimes disconcerting memoir *The Argonauts,* Maggie Nelson describes her impending motherhood: "I had nearly four decades to become myself before experimenting with my obliteration."

Motherhood as an "obliteration." Maggie was forty when she gave birth; I had just turned twenty-two. I didn't think of motherhood as an "obliteration." My term of choice would be "infection." A virus, or something like it, takes over and you can't shake it off for many years, perhaps decades. When something is obliterated, it leaves no traces. All has vanished. But motherhood carries a specific kind of visibility. Your body changes: the dreaded weight gain, the redistribution of fat, stretch marks, the changes in genitals and breasts, the disruption of sleep, hormonal blasts that affect every cell and organ, new bodily fluids emerging on their own schedule. Worse is the mental and emotional takeover, as it is deeper and more long-lasting than the physical. Something that wasn't *you* before your pregnancy has now set up shop in your body, mind, and heart and intends to stick around for a while. Perhaps the word I want is "invasion." Perhaps the "something" that invades is love?

On November 10, 1970, at 6:00 p.m., I was Sibbie. On November 11, 1970, at 5:30 p.m., I was a MOTHER. The long, painful tattoo of labor, a literal blood exchange if all goes well, had occurred. "I did it with my body!" to quote Anne Bradstreet in John Berryman's poem. Biology had made the word flesh, and the flesh of a mother is marked forever with linguistic distinction: *bad mother, good mother, working mother, unmarried mother* . . . there are many mothers, it seems, as many as our culture needs at any given time.

Sylvia Plath was a mother. She and I share a first name. We would soon share a connection with *Mademoiselle* magazine as well: in 1953, she served as a guest editor for the magazine's college issue, and nineteen years later, I won the magazine's annual college poetry prize, my first paying publication. My experience of motherhood, despite its stifling social expectations and bruising hours, inspired me to write poetry, and as with many other women of my generation, the poetry of Plath and Anne Sexton inspired me to investigate, swoon about, or rail against the wonders and indignities of being female.

Those were the warm and cuddly days, before adjectives were applied to my mothering, and before I irrevocably changed our family dynamic. My poems were full of the wonders of being a woman and my marveling at the small, perfect body of my daughter. My prize-winning poem begins *Women / are like flowers / they collect at corners / grow out of sidewalks.* I was imbued with solidarity, rooted to something larger than myself, something I felt very personally. It was a hopeful poem.

I wrote about childbirth, how *everything comes out except that smiling fist.* When Kim was three months old, she contracted roseola, and I stayed up all night with her on my lap until her fever broke. Later I wrote: *I waited with the stars / the insomniac beetles and birds . . . / I waited for my child / her eyes blind as marbles / to turn over / clean and fever free.* As a toddler, Kim was *you of the high slit / the corn cob legs,* a miniature Zena. But after my divorce, the poems changed. Now Kim has *a suitcase dragging where a doll should be / . . . victim of our haggling sprees.*

When Kim became an adolescent, my prize-winning poem had morphed into ones like this:

> Girls crowd the corner,
> a young forest of legs
> and shiny hair.
> They gossip.
> They giggle.
> Their pockets rounding.
>
> All in all they resemble grasses
> askew with summer.
>
> They will be here this August
> and next
> and the next
> watching their nipples.
>
> Then the world will rain
> down on them:
> they will spread out for shelter
> and find there is none.

Finally, after my life became more settled, my poetry became less caustic, and in a poem called "Faith," I wrote of a daily ritual I performed until Kim was a teenager. I was not obliterated when I walked up the staircase to her bedroom; love had, as it should, become a habit:

> My daughter sleeps. I bend to kiss her cheek
> but she is far away, the kiss a snowflake melting
> in the air.
> I smooth her hair back from her face or smooth

the air between her face and mine.
She does not know I come to do these things,
the small blank kindnesses of sleep.

Sean Ono Lennon also inspired John. In a remarkable creative arc, John went from writing songs about being a Nowhere Man and going cold turkey off drugs to singing about the simple joys of putting his son to bed. "Beautiful Boy" widened the repertoire not only of John's oeuvre but of popular songs in general. It's not the first song he wrote about being a father. On the *White Album,* the closing cut is "Good Night," a lullaby John had sung to Julian. But on the album, Ringo sings it with string accompaniment, an arrangement that depersonalizes its lyrics. Critic Tim Riley is correct when he calls the song "smarmy," and many listeners thought it might be a put-on. You can't blame them for thinking this, as many of the songs on the 1968 *White Album* are not sung "straight" but are satires or criticisms, such as "Sexy Sadie," "Piggies" and "Glass Onion."

However, twelve years later, on *Double Fantasy,* John sings "Beautiful Boy" straight—straight from his heart and directly to Sean's. "Beautiful Boy" is not as musically interesting as "Watching the Wheels," another *Double Fantasy* cut, which is a domesticated revision of *Revolver's* "I'm Only Sleeping." What "Beautiful Boy" does have is a startling emotional dimension, an almost embarrassing combination of simplicity and sincerity directed toward a subject one doesn't automatically associate with the hard-rocking, primal-screaming, truth-seeking John Lennon. Popular music doesn't have too many good songs about children. Most are overdone, loaded with religious or cultural subtexts, like "Scarlet Ribbons" or Perry Como's hit "Father of Girls," but "Beautiful Boy" bypasses all that. Sean is a toddler, all body and budding imagination, and John's song focuses on that. It's a sweet, sweet song.

My stand for feminist principles in 1973 almost cost me custody of my daughter, but when John Lennon became a feminist, the world took notice. Becoming a "mother" made John a better father, sadly not to Julian, but certainly to Sean. For almost five years after Sean's birth, John gave no public performances, made no records or traveled for professional reasons. Yoko handled all the business. His job and his delight was his son.

Can we claim that John and Yoko's reversal of gender roles began a social and economic trend that today no longer seems cutting edge? That's one valid way of looking at it. John's actual, as opposed to universal, revolution was domestic, conducted within the small private sphere of the family, where real social change often takes place. Some could diminish John's decision to become a househusband by raising class issues: the rich can afford to stay home, hire help, and ignore problems that would cause ordinary parents to tear out their hair. Some believe that John's domestic years were a sham and that instead of caring for Sean, he got depressed, stayed in his room, and went back on drugs. Even Julian discounts John's commitment to fatherhood by stating he never saw him bake bread or do domestic chores involving Sean when he visited John and Yoko in their New York apartment.

Nevertheless, no one should doubt John's commitment to his second family. In the photos and home movies, his face shows the total joy he feels toward Sean. Though just five when John died, Sean remembers his father vaguely but fondly. Body bits mostly: his father's ponytail, his ankles, his chin stubble. Sean's most vivid memory is of John's voice, "the first voice I ever heard . . . the first voice I ever heard speak English. It's the voice from which I learned to speak English." This declaration gives a new twist to the phrase "mother tongue."

John gave his body and his time to Sean, which is a beautiful thing for a father to do. Unlike Sean, however, Julian felt the absence of his father's body and was afraid of John's voice. One son suffers, one benefits. We cannot excuse John's negligence of Julian; it shaped Julian's decision never to have children himself, to stop the future from repeating the past. Yet beauty can also come from such desolation: Julian insisting he fly alone to New York to be with Sean after John was killed, the seventeen-year-old offering comfort to the five-year-old, brothers bonding through a painful confusion neither was prepared to understand. Or the beauty of my ex-husband at ten playing with his cars in the driveway on the day of his father's funeral, feeling a loss he could not understand, yet becoming a loving father himself. We need to remember that John Lennon was once a beautiful boy, one whose mother sang to him, but whose father, Alf, was just a shadow, never a body.

A month after John's death, Bob Christgau wrote that "Politically, [John's] indelible value was the way the abrasive anger that always lay just beneath his surface was transmuted into joy and hope." Becoming a househusband was John's most indelible political act because it helped create a new model of fatherhood, one that inspired men to be more joyful and present dads. During the last five years of his life, John finally had a home and love and peace. When Sean arrived, John became both joyful and present. The beautiful boy had created a beautiful man. But in the end, nothing in this world could keep the man with the ponytail and the one-in-a-million voice safe—not his sons, not his wives, not any of us.

AND IN THE END

How do you keep a dream alive when the dream is over? John Lennon knows something about ending dreams. His song "God" is a drum-filled litany of all he no longer believes in, including the Beatles. He concludes in believing only in himself: *"just me / Yoko and me . . . / the dream is over."*

In the spring of 1970, approximately six months before "God" was recorded for his first post-Beatles album, John, Yoko, and Jann Wenner, cofounder of *Rolling Stone,* sat in a near-empty San Francisco movie theater and watched *Let It Be,* the recently released documentary that features the band's rooftop concert atop Apple Studio in London. That January 30, 1969, concert was the last time the Beatles performed live, and arguably it is their best live performance.

There's no way of knowing what John was thinking while he watched the film, but by its end he was weeping. Watching his mates shivering and laughing on that cold rooftop must have been heartbreaking, and "God" may have originated in that near-empty theater, as John habitually wrote lyrics that expressed his pain. The song is a culmination; John had been dismantling the dream for some time. The Beatles stopped touring in 1966; he divorced and remarried, and he no longer believed in the deities who helped shape the 1960s—Buddha, Kennedy, and Zimmerman (Bob Dylan). It was time to move on.

Strange as it seems, when I think of John watching that movie, I think of Henry Adams seventy years earlier standing before the huge, humming dynamo in the Gallery of Machines at the Great Exposition in Paris. As Adams stared up at the hulking dynamo, he felt "his historical neck broken." In "The Virgin and the Dynamo," Adams's essay about the exhibition, he experienced the "abysmal fractures" within historical time along with "the sudden irruption of forces totally new." An entire historical period, a millennium of unity, had ceased, and the pain of the future, one dedicated to speed, efficiency, and science, would replace it. Adams didn't mention celebrity culture as part of this future, but he would have fully understood George Harrison's remark that the Beatles' "audience gave their money and their screams. But we gave our nervous systems." John's remark that "Carrying the Beatles or the Sixties dream around all your life is like carrying the Second World War" would have also registered with Henry Adams. It seems that whatever side you're on—the makers of the new or the loyalists to the past—history can hurt.

My historical neck was broken one summer day in 2018 at my local post office. It was only 9:30 in the morning, but the clerk behind the counter didn't look so good. While the postal clerk weighed my envelopes, I asked her, "Do you have any John Lennon stamps?"

"Who?"

"John Lennon." I wasn't about to explain.

"John Len . . . Lenno . . . Lennon . . . Lennon . . ." Her face unscrunched with a synaptic click that relaxed her perplexed eyebrows. "We have singer stamps, Elvis . . ." gesturing behind her to a bulletin board displaying an array of small faces, birds, and airplanes.

"I suppose Lennon's hasn't been issued yet," I said.

This was my neck-breaking moment—the clerk didn't immediately know who John Lennon was. Amid the mailers and packing tape, the Most Wanted posters, Adams's spirit did a little what-did-you-expect jig to remind me what I had forgotten: time marches on with its great eraser. Though I find it incredible that any adult wouldn't know who John Lennon was or who the Beatles were, I must accept that such people exist, and probably in large numbers.

And it's just not older postal workers who worry me. What are the Beatles to someone who listens to hip-hop or any of the other contemporary styles of music I know nothing about? The future always belongs to the young and to their market forces. After rapper Kendrick Lamar won the 2018 Pulitzer Prize for music, journalist Marc Weingarten gleefully announced the end of rock, zeroing in on the death of guitar-focused music and the gray heads who play it. He claimed hip-hop speaks to our era, which it undoubtedly might, but an era is much longer than one generation, and it will be interesting to see what musical trends evolve or even survive in our fast-changing culture. Whether intended or not, somewhere in Weingarten's spit-on-your-grave polemic is the unvoiced thought that the Beatles are kaput, for who else in the history of popular music began an era of such ongoing significance if not the Beatles?

One day either Paul McCartney or Ringo Starr will die, though Yoko, who's older, might precede them. Any of these deaths will create a resurgence of interest, a splurge of photographs, dribbles of certain songs, tributes, quotations, and magazine covers. These deaths will also recycle the 1980 death and legacy of John Lennon. Then what? Nothing lasts very long in this culture without suffering drastic changes, receding in relevance or congealing into a PBS coffee mug. I fear this is the Beatles' future, one that's both misty and porcelain hard. They *are* part of capital-letter History and always will be, but that doesn't guarantee recognition or relevance. And it certainly doesn't ensure that students learning about the Beatles' music will become passionate fans, though it's nice to think they would. Like everything else in this culture, a syllabus is open to change.

How do I keep a dream alive if that dream is over? As the future speeds on, as the paragraphs get shorter and shorter, and intelligence becomes more "artificial" and music more mechanical, Henry Adams's ghost hovers. Poor, sad ghost.

I imagine that John felt a profound loneliness while watching *Let It Be*. Loneliness compounded with happiness, for in the film John looks quite happy, as does Paul. Not everyone can literally watch a portion of their life up on a large screen. It's an absolute then/now moment, and sitting next to John was Yoko, the prime conduit for his movement from *then* to *now*. Whatever History had in store for John and the Beatles, no one could rob him of his right to say *I was there*.

And no one can rob me of that either.

The snapshot I took of John standing on Ed Sullivan's stage retains a great mystery for me. What did I see in that micromoment beforehand to make me snap the shutter when I did? Without knowing anything about photography, I had fixed John in a triangle of visibility between a cameraman's back and the studio's overhead lights. The more I look at this photograph, the more I see entrapment—the white walls, the looming camera, the hot lights—just a few of the restraints that represented John's life as a Beatle in 1965. And if John wasn't actually singing in my photograph, what was he doing? Did I capture the grind and fakery of endless tours singing the same songs before screaming audiences? The next day, Sunday, August 15th, playing Shea Stadium before a crowd of 55,000, the band couldn't hear each other, but they knew the songs well enough to perform them. One year later, at Candlestick Park in San Francisco, the Beatles put an end to their touring years. This chronology imbues my photograph with a pathos I could not have predicted when I took it. It marks a historical turning point. *Rubber Soul* awaited, then *Revolver* and *Sgt. Pepper's Lonely Hearts Club Band*. Freed from touring, the Beatles could create their music without the dismal obligations of the road. They could become themselves. And this becoming themselves led to the band's demise, the end of the dream. It would now be up to the fans, the listeners, the newbies hearing their parents' copy of *Rubber Soul* for the first time, to keep alive their music, to understand their importance and to love them.

I wonder now if looking at John's photograph might have been the start of this book you've been reading. One night I opened up a little drawer, dug around among some incidental papers, found the envelope, opened it, and, well . . . could I help keep the dream alive?

So I began writing. But I also knew there'd come a reckoning. After all my reading and listening, all the contrary fact-checking and confusion; after the sleepless nights when a song or two or three swept through my brain instead of silly dreams; after the second and third guessing; after batting away the lingering past humiliations and uncertainties, I arrived at one overwhelming question: *who would want to read about me?*

So I answered my question. I understood the importance of loving what I love, of following a hunch, of holding true to a thoughtful take on the matter. Of evolving through both the ecstasy and the exhaustion of one's subject. I thought about taking on "the boys," not the Beatles but their male critics. I did that once before, in an academic setting, when dear, dear Hemingway flooded my bloodstream with his prose and sad biography. Back then, some of the boys didn't like what I did with their Hemingway, but they got over it. Now, with the Beatles, it wasn't a matter of spelunking the multiple rifts in gender politics in service of dismantling the male myth; no, it would be more housebound than that, more *personal*, out of the classroom and into the record cabinets of freaks like me, into the bibliographies, the discographies, the Internet connections of thoughtful listeners only to find out there was just too much. I had to recede and crawl back up the beach lest the tide take me out.

Thoughtful. Hopeful. Private. Secure. In thrall. This is what I became. These Beatles that I'd write about would be *mine.*

What I'm riffing on is *experience*—who has it, whose counts, what constitutes a *readable* experience. Where is the fifteen-year-old girl in all this, that transfixed teenager standing in the middle of the street one rainy December night? What about the overwhelmed twenty-something mom who put childish toys away, who crossed over into Black music only to reverse course and rejoin the dystopian America of Steely Dan, a young mother who identified as a poet but never quite mastered any of it, because she was gravity bound, willingly, by such tasks as keeping the fridge clean and buying good shoes for her daughter who has such lovely, strong feet—ballerina feet? This lonely, frightened mother who carved out some edges but kept them dusted, and those edges did and sometimes didn't include John Lennon and the Beatles, though they were always in the house, in record cabinets and desks, in folders creased with memory, in photographs, and on shelves filled with books and small objects of private importance. This mother cultivated a life. She was grateful, she never forgot what mattered, her father's trombone, her mother's piano, her sister's voice, her brother, all the various rooms that had made a difference, every little thing. She followed her hunches, throwing out theories while wiping down the spines of books she bought as a teenager and never got around to reading.

What could this woman possibly have to say?

Picture a dinner party, a real one, two years ago. Eight lovely people—Vassar, Stanford, Harvard, I forget the others—years spent traveling the globe, shaking hands with

John Kerry, landing spectacularly but safely in third-world airports. Multiple languages at their beck and call, along with knowing all the different kinds of schnapps. I listened and sank. It was not the first time I'd been in such a position. Sitting at a long table often makes me feel small. Across the table, experienced in his own way, The Man I Love sat quietly. He wasn't sinking. He doesn't let things bother him like they bother me.

The table suddenly grew quiet. Then I took a step into unsupported air, just as the Zen posters tell you to do, and I said, "I saw the Beatles at the Ed Sullivan studio in August 1965."

It was as though I had caused the table to levitate. Forks gently resumed their original places; all eyes, as though sequenced to widen simultaneously, turned to me. The woman on my left, a lovely gal wearing laddered tights and killer boots, and on retainer at the UN, said in a voice she hadn't used since she was thirteen, "You did!" At that moment I knew I would begin: a door opened and I stepped through it.

JOHN LENNON IS SHOT TO DEATH, DECEMBER 8, 1980

He once said death is like leaving one car
and getting into another, and this is the night he does it,
out of the limo and into the cop car—
curb service, exactly like he said it'd be.

How many steps between them? Four? Five? Little life
details pushing through him that rain-ruined night.
His ruined life raining on the seat.

Something's wailing in the doorway. That woman . . .

Now we know how many holes it took—
now we know who counted them—

Days before, he dreamed of Liverpool, school ties and tea sets.
Sorry, old boy, nothin' doin.'
Your guitars will be auctioned, your face will flicker
in all the old familiar places—
though beauty will be temporarily out of service.

Oh Johnny Boy, Oh Johnny Boy, what dark night called you back to those cold stones and cellar music?

It's you must go, and we must bide.

AUG   65   •

PHOTO BY SIBBIE O'SULLIVAN ©

ACKNOWLEDGMENTS

Many thanks to Ron Charles, Nora Krug, and Stephanie Merry, my editors at the *Washington Post*. A special thank you to Dennis Drabelle, also of the *Post,* who liked what I had to say and let me say it. I won't forget your thoughtfulness and generosity.

The crew at Mad Creek Books was fabulous and a joy to work with. My heartfelt thanks to all of you: Kristen A. Elias Rowley, Taralee Cyphers, Juliet Williams, Rebecca Bostock, David Lazar, and Patrick Madden.

Thanks to those I interviewed or consulted for this book: Bob Hitchcock, Rita Schreiber, and novelist Sarah Pleydell. Special thanks to novelist Keith Donohue for his encouragement. A big hug to Jackson Bryer, a great and honest reader. My pal Jonathan Auerbach for his encouragement and humor. Writer and filmmaker George Pelecanos for his honesty and friendship. Marilyn Mark, thanks for urging me forward. To Melanie Donohue for her keen eye. The Ladies, to whom I've dedicated this book, were central in its becoming. Thank you for your love, your appraisals, and your support. To Ruth Sievers, for being the blessing you are.

To Betty, my old friend. My experience of the Beatles would have been much less were it not for your friendship, your parents' generosity, and the raucous good times we had as teenagers.

My brother, Ron Croy, a wonderful ally. My daughter, Kim O'Sullivan, for her many gifts, both material and spiritual. If my sister Marlene were alive, I'd ask her to sing us all a song.

Finally, to my partner Robbie. In the words of Steely Dan: *You walked in / And my life began again.*

SELECTED BIBLIOGRAPHY

Bangs, Lester. *Psychotic Reactions and Carburetor Dung.* Ed. Greil Marcus. New York: Alfred A. Knopf, 1988.

Christgau, Robert and John Piccarella. "Portrait of the Artist as a Rock and Roll Star." *The Ballad of John and Yoko.* Eds. Jonathan Cott and Christine Doudna. New York: Rolling Stone Press Book, 1982.

Christgau, Robert. *Going into the City: Portrait of a Critic as a Young Man.* New York: Dey Street Books, 2015.

Ehrenreich, Barbara, Elizabeth Hess and Gloria Jacobs. *Re-Making Love: The Feminization of Sex.* New York: Anchor Book, 1986.

Ford, Mark. "I gotta use words." *London Review of Books* 38.16 (11 August 2016): 9–12.

Hagan, Joe. *Sticky Fingers: The Life and Times of Jann Wenner and Rolling Stone Magazine.* New York: Alfred A. Knopf, 2017.

Kimsey, John. "Spinning the Historical Record: Lennon, McCartney, and Museum Politics." *Reading the Beatles, Cultural Studies, Literary Criticism, and the Fab Four.* Eds. Kenneth Womack and Todd F. Davis. Albany: State University of New York Press, 2006.

Lennon, Cynthia. *John.* New York: Three Rivers Press, 2005.

Lewisohn, Mark. *Tune In: The Beatles All These Years, Volume 1.* New York: Crown Archetype, 2013.

―――. *The Complete Beatles Chronicle.* London: Hamlyn, 2005.

MacDonald, Ian. *Revolution in the Head: The Beatles' Records and the Sixties.* 3rd ed. Chicago: Chicago Review Press, 2005.

Marcus, Greil. *The History of Rock 'N' Roll in Ten Songs.* New Haven: Yale University Press, 2014.

McKinney, Devin. *Magic Circles: The Beatles in Dream and History.* Cambridge: Harvard University Press, 2003.

Nelson, Maggie. *The Argonauts.* Minneapolis: Graywolf Press, 2015.

Norman, Philip. *John Lennon: The Life.* New York: Ecco, 2008.

―――. *Shout! The Beatles in Their Generation.* 3rd ed. New York: Simon and Schuster, 2003.

O'Brien. Geoffrey. *Sonata for Jukebox.* New York: Counterpoint, 2004.

Reynolds, Simon. *Retromania: Pop Culture's Addiction to Its Own Past.* New York: Farrar, Straus and Giroux, 2011.

Riley, Tim. *Tell Me Why: A Beatles Commentary.* Cambridge: De Capo, 2002.

Sawyers, June Skinner, ed. *Read the Beatles: Classic and New Writings on the Beatles, Their Legacy, and Why They Still Matter.* New York: Penguin Books, 2006.

Sheff, David. *All We Are Saying: The Last Major Interview with John Lennon and Yoko Ono.* New York: St. Martin's Griffin, 1981.

Thomson, Elizabeth and David Gutman, eds. *The Lennon Companion Twenty-five Years of Comment.* Cambridge: De Capo, 2004.

Turner, Steve. *The Beatles A Hard Day's Write: The Story Behind Every Song.* New York: MJF Books, 1994.

Wenner, Jann S. *Lennon Remembers.* New York: Verso, 2000.

Willis, Ellen. *Out of the Vinyl Deeps: Ellen Willis on Rock Music.* Ed. Nona Willis Aronowitz. Minneapolis: University of Minnesota Press, 2011.

There are many good online sites for the Beatles. One of my favorites is the Beatles Bible: https.//www.beatlesbible.com.

21ST CENTURY ESSAYS

David Lazar and Patrick Madden, Series Editors

This series from Mad Creek Books is a vehicle to discover, publish, and promote some of the most daring, ingenious, and artistic nonfiction. This is the first and only major series that announces its focus on the essay—a genre whose plasticity, timelessness, popularity, and centrality to nonfiction writing make it especially important in the field of nonfiction literature. In addition to publishing the most interesting and innovative books of essays by American writers, the series publishes extraordinary international essayists and reprint works by neglected or forgotten essayists, voices that deserve to be heard, revived, and reprised. The series is a major addition to the possibilities of contemporary literary nonfiction, focusing on that central, frequently chimerical, and invariably supple form: The Essay.